To Phil.

From Irene.

Safeguard Coaches

OF GUILDFORD

Safeguard Coaches

OF GUILDFORD

A NINETIETH ANNIVERSARY CELEBRATION
OF A FAMILY BUSINESS

Laurie James

AMBERLEY

Front cover images provided by John Kaye and Optare Group.

First published 2014

Amberley Publishing
The Hill, Stroud
Gloucestershire, GL5 4EP

www.amberley-books.com

Copyright © Laurie James 2014

The right of Laurie James to be identified as the Author
of this work has been asserted in accordance with the
Copyrights, Designs and Patents Act 1988.

ISBN 978 1 4456 1690 2
Ebook ISBN 978 1 4456 1702 2

British Library Cataloguing in Publication Data.
A catalogue record for this book is available from the British Library.

Typeset in 10pt on 12pt Celeste OT.
Typesetting and Origination by Amberley Publishing.
Printed in the UK.

CONTENTS

Published to celebrate ninety years of Safeguard Coaches and five generations of family endeavour, March 2014

The directors of Safeguard Coaches Ltd in October 2013, left to right, Mark Newman, Jane Newman, Andrew Halliday, Therese Hunter and David Newman.

Four Bedford SB coaches lined up in North Street, Guildford at the Excursion departure point near the library in the early 1960s. Among the drivers, Bert Newman is third from the left. Note the contemporary Safeguard 'flag' device on the front of the coaches and the portable boards used to advertise that day's trips to the coast or countryside. (*Studio 57/ Safeguard Collection*)

FOREWORD BY THE DIRECTORS OF SAFEGUARD COACHES

We are most pleased to take this opportunity to pay tribute to Laurie James for all his hard work researching and writing an expanded history of Safeguard Coaches. Building on the 1984 book by John Sutton and Norman Hamshere, Laurie has unearthed previously forgotten information from Company archives, Council licensing records and other sources, woven the story of the family and Company together and incorporated many recollections and pictures of family members and staff as well as the vehicles operated over what is now an amazing ninety years of continuous operation.

We would also like to pay tribute to all the past and present staff associated with Safeguard Coaches. All have contributed, or are contributing, to the success of the Company and all can justifiably feel proud of Safeguard Coaches which for many has been a way of life rather than merely a job. We thank them all.

Reaching its ninetieth anniversary is a fantastic achievement for a Company which has been owned by members of the same family since its inception in 1924 and with a fifth generation now represented on its Board of Directors. However, we will not rest on our laurels but rather meet the challenges ahead and continue to provide excellent service to customers old and new for very many more years to come.

David Newman
Jane Newman
Mark Newman
Therese Hunter
Andrew Halliday

March 2014

ACKNOWLEDGEMENTS

This book would not have come to fruition in the form you see it without the support of Safeguard Coaches, its owners and its Managing Director. I am indebted to the latter – Andrew Halliday, for officially backing this project to record the company's history and to mark its ninetieth anniversary. Andrew has acted as a channel for information from various sources, not least from the surviving company archives, as well as supplying a perspective on activities since his arrival in 2000. He has also arranged or conducted interviews with members of the Newman family and members of staff, past and present, to capture some of their memories, as well as enabling the Safeguard and Newman family photographic archives to be available. Mark and David Newman have clarified some matters as well as supplying further archive material, some family photographs and vehicle photographs from the 1920s through to the 1990s. The late Gill Newman also contributed memories, whilst Gordon Button (former Traffic Manager and Company Secretary) shared his memories and his personal collection of photographs and documents. Long-serving drivers Alan Vineer, Brian Williams, Nigel Cotton, Malcolm Toghill and John Lake recalled the past, along with former conductress Betty Ball, as well as Joan Tubbs, who with her husband owned the shop adjacent to the Safeguard garage.

A firm starting point was provided by the booklet from 1984 written by Norman Hamshere and the late John Sutton. Some information on the years up to 1930 came from the Minutes of the Guildford Watch Committee and Woking Council's Omnibus Sub-Committee, held by the Surrey History Centre. These were transcribed by Peter Trevaskis and Alan Lambert, to whom I am once again grateful. For some vehicle information, acknowledgement goes to the PSV Circle and Keith Wheal. Keith, along with Richard Kirwin, has generously offered their photographic collections from which to select illustrations. Information on other aspects came from the late Dr Peter Holmes and Mike Stephens. Thanks must also be extended to the Omnibus Society (including its South Eastern Branch Bulletin), the *Surrey Advertiser* newspaper, the Census 1911 website and Surrey County Council's Passenger Transport Group. For some photographs, we were unable to identify the source, so in general these are credited to the supplier. Some of them have come from photo-sharing websites and contacting people has been challenging in certain cases. If anybody recognises their work which has not been correctly attributed, please accept apologies and/or get in touch via the Publisher. Some of the tickets are from the collections of Roger Atkinson and John King, to whom thanks are due.

Once again, many thanks to Campbell McCutcheon and all at Amberley Publishing for putting another of my projects into print and love and gratitude to my wife Michaela for her document management skills and for her support, despite gritting her teeth over 'another damn bus book'. As always, any error or omission is mine alone, for which I apologise in advance. If anybody can add to or correct anything in the book, I would be pleased if they came forward via the Publisher.

Laurie James, Walton on Thames 2014

INTRODUCTION

Guildford is the county town of Surrey, situated some twenty-seven miles south-west of central London at a strategic gap for communications carved by the River Wey in the North Downs range of hills. It has long been a commercial and shopping centre for a large hinterland and benefits from the A3 London–Portsmouth trunk road. Following the advent of railways, many of its residents have commuted daily to London and other employment centres. Since the last war, there has been significant housing estate growth on the outskirts. As well as being the home of Dennis (and successors) – well known motor vehicle manufacturers – there is now much light and high-tech industry in the town, as well as considerable office accommodation. There is also the Research Park, a major hospital, a cathedral and an extensive University of Surrey campus, with student numbers contributing to the growth of Guildford's population, so that by 2010 it stood at around 74,000.

In terms of formative road public transport, Guildford was on territorial boundary of two major providers – Aldershot & District Traction Co. Ltd and London General Omnibus Co. Ltd, with its subsidiary East Surrey Traction Co. Ltd. After the First World War these companies secured most of the strategic interurban bus routes, but the 1920s also saw a proliferation of small 'independent' operators providing either strong competition, or developing their own services. A number of such firms jockeyed for position and trade with the larger companies but the strongest player usually survived, although the Guildford Watch Committee (the town's licensing body) seemed sympathetic to locally-based entrepreneurs. The overall history of bus service development in Guildford is for another day, but into the cut throat operating environment of the 1920s, came the Newman Brothers.

Of all the bus operators active in Guildford in that era, Safeguard Coaches is a unique survivor. It still trades under the same name, is controlled by the founding family, retains its original depot site and still runs bus services to the same areas as those selected for its first routes back in 1927. It is one of the very few 'traditional' independent firms, dating back to the formative years of bus and coach operation, still active in the south of England.

Perhaps a reason for why the firm has survived all these years is the high quality service given by the Newman family and their staff to their customers, whether they were patrons of the day trips, extended holiday tours, the coastal express services, whether they were private hire customers, whether they contracted Safeguard to undertake regular trips or whether they were users of the bus services. The vehicles were (and are) always clean, well-presented and maintained to a high level. Astute, cost-effective and adaptable management of the business by the family and others has meant that it has been able to weather the challenges put upon it by various outside influences, including recessions, financial hardship for the owning family and the company, the exigencies of war, flooding, the rise of private motoring, predatory competition and 'deregulation' of the bus and coach industry, as well as policy changes and fiscal pressures created by politicians of all persuasions, both national and local. The happy-go-lucky charabanc era of the 1920s, cut-throat competition in the latter part of that decade, fifty years of rigid, stifling (but protective) licensing legislation from the 1930s, a struggle to rebuild after the war, a 'free market' for bus services since 1986 and more aggressive competition in the 1990s – Safeguard has seen them all.

Another factor influencing the longevity of Safeguard must be the exemplary way that they looked after their staff and continue to do so. Everybody who worked hard for the firm was rewarded by being embraced into the wider Safeguard 'family'. Almost without exception, long-term employees will say that the passengers were always loyal, through good and bad times and it was a great company to work for. No wonder it was hard to get a job with Safeguard, as in days gone by, very few people ever left its employ.

An excellent short history was written to commemorate Safeguard's sixtieth anniversary in 1984. Now it is time to celebrate the ninetieth anniversary of the firm, which has avoided takeover or departure from the industry, as so many other small bus and coach firms have been subjected to. In terms of research, more has been discovered regarding the early years and so much new has happened since 1984 – some of it unimaginable back then. The Newman family are rightly proud of their ownership spanning five generations (so far!), through good times and sad times. This book hopefully recognises and salutes their achievements and those of their loyal staff, past and present, as much as recording Safeguard's operations, vehicles and awareness of the company by its customers and local residents over the last ninety years. Safeguard should be viewed as part of Guildford's social history.

Above left: Outside their house at Ridgemount, we see the Newman family. Henry and Annie are seated front left and sons (left to right, back), Frank, Arthur, John and Albert, with Fred seated front right. (*Newman Family Collection*)

Above right: The children standing outside the Newman family home, 1 Ridgemount, are Bert and one of his brothers in the early 1900s. The outbuildings visible on the left may have been stables subsequently used by Arthur Newman for his horses. Ridgemount itself has a rough surface. Much later, no. 1 was occupied by Gordon Streeter and the adjacent no. 3 by Mr and Mrs Emmins. Today, this area is part of the Safeguard depot yard. This postcard was sent by Annie Newman to her mother, Mrs Pharo, in Upper Hale in 1910. (*Newman Family Collection*)

EARLY DAYS – BRICKS AND BUSES

Henry (or Harry) Newman was born at Hale near Farnham in 1859. Around 1884 he married Annie who was two years younger and came from the same district. Their first child, Ada, was also born at Hale. However, sons John Henry, Arthur Bryant, Frank, Frederick Herbert and Albert Harold were all born in Guildford. By the time of the 1911 census, the boys' ages ranged from eighteen to nine years and the family was living at Brickyard Cottage at the bottom of Ridgemount in Guildford. Although not far from the town centre and station, Ridgemount was just over the border with Artington Parish. In 1911 John Newman was a labourer at the brickyard while Arthur's occupation was given as Hairdresser's Apprentice. In view of later developments, Arthur's career was to change course after war service! Two of the sons are said to have been steeplejacks at one time.

Henry Newman was the manager or foreman of Mitchell's Brick Yard in Guildford Park and his home was originally owned by that firm. Today, the main area of the brick fields has been replaced by Guildford Park Avenue and the car park adjacent to the railway. Mitchell also owned a yard behind the cottage with stabling for horses, which pulled carts for delivering the bricks. During the First World War, Arthur Newman had been an officer in the Royal Flying Corps and after demobilisation, he established a coal delivery business there; eventually horses were replaced with motor vehicles, which were used for general haulage as well as coal deliveries. By the early 1920s, Arthur's brothers John, Fred and Bert were involved with his business. Farming was another activity and pigs and a couple of cows were kept on land nearby. Henry Newman died in 1923 but Annie continued to live at Brickyard Cottage at 1 Ridgemount.

Around that time, bales of straw were put in the back of a lorry to act as seating for a party of boy scouts who were taken to Bognor. En route in Sussex, everybody apparently had to get off and walk, in order that the vehicle could climb Bury Hill. In 1924 one of Arthur's vehicles – a Daimler Y type on solid tyres – sustained some accident damage at Woking. He was no doubt aware of the rise in the numbers of local firms (as well as the larger Aldershot & District Traction Co. and East Surrey Traction Co.) that had started bus services or were offering pleasure trips by charabanc. He used the Daimler's misfortune as an opportunity to diversify, by replacing its truck body with that of a twenty-eight-seat charabanc, painted maroon. This was available for hire and for pleasure trips to the coast, being driven by Fred Newman. Its registration number is not confirmed but may have been PB 9977. By 1926 a Berliet fourteen-seat and two Chevrolet fourteen-seat charabancs were in use. These were apparently silver or silver and red in colour and carried a 'HN' monogram on their sides, signifying Mrs Henry Newman. The business was expanding, with day trips in summer being advertised to Brighton, Worthing, Bognor and Littlehampton (fare 6s) and to Sandown Park Races at Esher (fare 3s 6d). Activities were being marketed as 'The Safeguard Coaches', with bookings being carried out at Arthur's private address – Ottorose, 8 Agraria

This view of a charabanc is in the Newman family collection. Although unconfirmed as such, this might be Arthur Newman's first charabanc in 1924, on a former lorry chassis by Daimler. On the thin, solid tyres, with the road conditions of the time, a trip to the coast would have been challenging on the posterior, but eagerly participated in. (*Safeguard Collection*)

Road – as well as at agents in Guildford and Godalming. Annie Newman assisted with administrative matters, Bert Newman was also driving, while Arthur dealt with vehicle maintenance, being an excellent mechanic.

Some ambiguity applies to two more Chevrolets which by June 1926 were licensed by Guildford Corporation, bearing registration numbers PF 1837/8. Photographic evidence c.1927 shows them as having saloon bus bodywork, but local licensing records describe them as 'charabanc' in June 1926 and as 'bus' in October 1927. The earlier reference may just signify that they were not originally licensed for bus service work and no physical change was made. However, things were soon to alter in respect of bus operations.

Newman Brothers were undertaking haulage of building materials in connection with the new Aldershot Road Estate, on land to the south of that road. Bert Newman actually delivered the first lorry load of timber to the site in early 1927. Once some houses were finished and occupied, there would be a need for a bus service. At that time, Aldershot & District (A&D) service 20 (Guildford–Aldershot) ran along the Aldershot Road and had been joined on 25 June 1926 by service 31A (Puttenham–Compton–Guildford–Wood Street Green), which turned off at Clock House. The latter service was probably started to compete with Crouch's service to Wood Street and there was also a low-frequency service out to Normandy and Wanborough run by Messrs. Cartland and Baker.

On 2 September 1927, Arthur Newman wrote to the Town Clerk to apply to run a bus service to the new 'Corporation Housing Estate' from Guildford (North Street) via Woodbridge Road, Woodbridge Hill, Weston Road, Beckingham Road and Aldershot Road, terminating at the Aldershot Road Flats near Woodside at the north end of the future Southway Avenue. A frequency of three journeys per hour was suggested on weekdays, with a service as required on Sunday afternoons, commencing on 18 October 1927 at a through single fare of 3d. The Watch Committee

Right: Two Chevrolet fourteen-seat charabancs with bodywork by REAL arrived in 1926, with pneumatic tyres. This type of vehicle, with a folding canvas hood, was commonplace at that time. Note the shield insignia with the 'HN' (representing Mrs Henry Newman) monogram. (*Author's Collection*)

Below left: Seen in the Safeguard yard, with its old sheds, is the complete bus service fleet, probably in late 1927. PF 1837/8 were fourteen-seaters from 1926, while PH 4809 is a twenty-seat six-wheeler. All are Chevrolets with REAL bodywork and all are labelled for the original service to the Aldershot Road Estate Flats via Weston Road. (*Author's Collection*)

Below right: This is a closer view of one of the 1926 Chevrolet buses, typical of the type of vehicle used by many small operators in the UK during the 1920s. They were quite sprightly and compact – ideal for getting in front of heavier and slower-moving Aldershot & District (A&D) buses. (*Safeguard Collection*)

had approved the application by the middle of September, so the service probably started earlier than anticipated. It was initiated with Chevrolets PF 1837/8, which were joined by October 1927 by PH 4809, a six-wheel three-axle Chevrolet with twenty seats. The latter disgraced itself one day by returning to Guildford on only five wheels, the sixth having become detached and overtaken the bus when going down Woodbridge Hill.

No doubt encouraged by the outcome, Arthur Newman applied successfully in mid-November 1927 to extend the service across Guildford to The Chase in Guildford Park Estate, passing Ridgemount on its way. Aldershot & District had also been serving Guildford Park, terminating at The Oval since 14 May 1925, when their service 27 (Merrow–Guildford) was extended. The competitive arrival of Safeguard was probably viewed with irritation. To protect their position on the Aldershot Road, A&D had started a supplementary service 20C to the Aldershot Road Estate, as early as 6 October 1927. Safeguard were running every fifteen minutes. Thus A&D and Safeguard were in conflict on both that route and the one to Guildford Park. Meanwhile, further houses had been built and Southway Avenue extended, although it was still a cul-de-sac. By the end of April 1928, Safeguard was running to the far end of that road, after requests from the Housing Committee and A&D followed suit very soon afterwards. Both Fred and Bert Newman were to occupy houses close to each other in Southway Avenue. By autumn 1928, more buses were needed by Safeguard, so the two Chevrolet charabancs had their bodies replaced with new fourteen-seat saloon bus bodywork made by Slough Quality – these were reregistered as PH 7996/7 and licensed in December 1928.

As the instigator of the Aldershot Road Estate service, the Newmans regarded A&D as an interloper and now set their sights on a route where A&D was long-established and dominant. In September 1928 they applied to Guildford's Chief Constable and Godalming Town Council to run between those two towns on the direct route along Portsmouth Road through St. Catherines, Peasmarsh and Farncombe Meadrow, every twenty minutes. A&D ran frequently on their services 21, 21A and 22, so it was impossible to devise a schedule that totally avoided the A&D timings. Godalming Town Council refused the application in October, as they did not wish to see any additional buses licensed in their area. However, the Guildford Watch Committee did show some concern at this constraint on a local business. A meeting between the two Councils was arranged for 5 December to discuss the licensing of buses in general. However, having sufficient spare bus licenses in the area, A&D just went ahead on 7 December 1928 with a supplementary service 22A from Guildford along the Portsmouth Road to Farncombe Station via Hare Lane and The Oval. Safeguard had already re-applied but this time proposed to divert their route through Farncombe via Church Road, The Oval (not to be confused with the one in Guildford), Summers Road, Farncombe Street, Nightingale Road and Borough Road, opening up some new links from a residential area. Thus, the reason for A&D's hasty action was clear.

At Godalming Town Council on 1 January 1929, some councillors thought that A&D had a monopoly which was unfair to the 'small man'. Although licenses had previously been granted to A&D for additional buses, the Council should be able to approve specific service applications. Others spoke in favour of A&D and the need for a cohesive local bus service. Late in that month, Godalming Council refused Safeguard's revised application too, which led to a similar decision from Guildford. Safeguard lodged an appeal with the Minister of Transport and an inquiry was held in Godalming on 22 March 1929, where it emerged that half of the fifty bus licenses granted to A&D in Godalming Borough were not being used except for duplication at busy times. A petition from Farncombe with 100 signatures was presented in support of Safeguard running thence to Godalming. The Borough Surveyor said the proposed route was dangerous with some steep gradients, to which Arthur

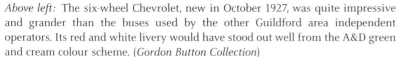

Above left: The six-wheel Chevrolet, new in October 1927, was quite impressive and grander than the buses used by the other Guildford area independent operators. Its red and white livery would have stood out well from the A&D green and cream colour scheme. (*Gordon Button Collection*)

Above right: The two 1926 Chevrolet charabancs were re-bodied by Slough Quality in 1928 as fourteen-seat saloon buses and given new registration marks, so that more vehicles were available for the local services. PH 7997 appears to be at the bottom of Ridgemount, near the yard entrance. (*Author's Collection*)

Right: By the late 1920s, charabanc style vehicles were becoming unfashionable as passengers demanded better comfort on longer trips. Safeguard updated their fleet with two Chevrolet fourteen-seat 'all weather' coaches, with side windows and folding canvas roofs that could be folded back in good weather. (*Safeguard Collection*)

Newman responded by saying that his buses had four wheel brakes and there were cross roads and turnings on any bus route. There was a disagreement between Alderman Brown and Safeguard's advocate over what constituted a monopoly. It was pointed out that at a similar inquiry in 1925 the Ministry had upheld the Council's decision not to license another operator. In April 1929, Safeguard suffered the same outcome, with the Appeal being dismissed.

Safeguard took delivery of another Chevrolet bus in March 1929 (PK 7173) to strengthen capacity at busy times. However, Guildford Watch Committee would only license it as a 'standby' vehicle, for use when another bus was off the road. By the latter part of the 1920s, the open charabanc style of vehicle was falling out of fashion, being replaced with all-weather coaches, with a folding canvas roof for fine days. For their coach activities, Safeguard purchased two Chevrolets with such bodywork – YW 3286 in June 1928 and PK 9505 in spring 1929. Excursions were still advertised, with evening Mystery Drives involving a stop at a public house being very popular. The beauty spot of Newlands Corner, high on the North Downs near Guildford, had many visitors at weekends and in April 1929 Safeguard was granted a licence to run a shuttle service from Guildford via Merrow on Sunday and Bank Holiday afternoons. This decision was extremely unpopular with A&D, East Surrey, Tillingbourne Valley and Magnet Omnibus, who already served Newlands Corner and feared their trade would be abstracted.

Undeterred by the Godalming experience, Safeguard applied in April 1929 to extend the Guildford Park service to Onslow Village via Elmside and Hedgeway; this was granted. A&D already ran to Onslow Village via Farnham Road (service 30) but introduced a further competitive service 27A from 30 April 1929, from Guildford to Onslow Village via Guildford Park. The battle for trade would be intense, employing cut-throat measures on both the Onslow Village and Aldershot Road routes. On the

latter, A&D reduced their fares on service 20C on 19 April 1929 from *3d* single, *5d* return for a full journey, to a ridiculously uneconomic rate of 1*d* flat fare single or return for a round trip of six miles, so Safeguard reduced theirs too. However, Arthur Newman said that *3d* return was the lowest price at which he could afford to run. Both Safeguard and A&D were running every ten minutes with A&D having increased the frequency of service 20C from every twenty minutes using new buses and reduced fares as 'an experiment'. Despite higher fares, Safeguard retained a good degree of customer loyalty. Letters appeared in the *Surrey Advertiser* newspaper in support of the 'small man' and fair play, criticising A&D's attempts to force a capitulation from small operators such as Safeguard and also Tillingbourne Valley in respect of the Guildford–Chilworth route. If A&D were to gain a monopoly, fares would soon go up to a level higher than the original.

A resident of Onslow Village complained to the Town Clerk that there were sixteen buses an hour passing his house, many of them empty. This added to wear and tear on the estate roads and caused 'disturbance to the peace and amenities of the village by the sound of braking, gear changing, hooting and reverberation. Is it not possible to treat this (bus war) as a public nuisance and have it stopped? Buses entering Onslow Village from Guildford Park should turn at the junction of Hedgeway and Bannisters Road, where those entering from Farnham Road also turn, obviating some of the overlapping'.

In July 1929, Safeguard applied again for a Guildford–Farncombe– Godalming service, as part of their battle with A&D. The Chief Constable recommended that the Watch Committee refuse the application as he felt that there were sufficient services over the route and that congestion in Park Street, Guildford would be worsened by additional bus movements. On 13 September 1929, Arthur Newman applied for a number of new services in a blatant competitive strike against well-established A&D routes, which if they had been granted would have required a large increase in fleet size. These were: Guildford–Wood Street–Normandy–Ash–Aldershot (every thirty minutes), Guildford–Stoke–Mayford–Kingfield Green–Woking (three journeys per hour) and Guildford–Stoughton (Royal Hotel) via Manor Road (every fifteen minutes, also competing with Yellow Bus Services). All of them were promptly refused by the Watch Committee, leading to a further batch of applications the following month. Newman suggested that the late Chief Constable had encouraged him to apply for new services in view of the difficult time he was having with his town services. These were: Guildford–Boxgrove Road–Burpham–Merrow–Guildford (every thirty minutes), Guildford–Stoke–Cemetery Road–Grange Road (every fifteen minutes) and Guildford–St. Catherines–Peasmarsh–Shalford–Guildford (every thirty minutes). These were also refused.

Aldershot & District revised their fares to the Aldershot Road Estate from 21 October 1929, to give a single fare of 2d and a return of 3d, matching Safeguard's return fare. However, the new Safeguard applications and perhaps some Watch Committee encouragement seems to have prompted an opening of negotiations between Safeguard and A&D, leading to an agreement to restore commercial common sense and the status quo. Henceforth, Safeguard would solely run to Aldershot Road Estate (by then known as Westborough, with a terminus at Foxburrows Avenue) every ten minutes, while A&D would solely serve Onslow Village via Farnham Road. Both firms would share the service out to Guildford Park, each running every thirty minutes. Fares would be stabilised at around 1d per mile. Thus, after 18 December 1929, A&D services 20C and 27A were withdrawn and Safeguard's Onslow Village service was curtailed at Guildford Park, complementing A&D service 27.

Safeguard took delivery in January 1930 of a larger capacity bus in the form of a twenty-nine-seat Graham Dodge with Thurgood body, registered PG 5320. This was purchased through Puttocks in Guildford and was the first Safeguard bus to be painted predominantly red, as became familiar. Safeguard also asked permission from the Council to erect bus shelters at their own expense in Weston Road and Southway Avenue.

Not everybody was happy with the removal of buses from the lower end of Onslow Village. An anonymous letter from a resident to the Town Clerk said people now had to walk home in the rain from the Bannisters Road terminus and asked for a service to be restored along Old Palace Road. It continued 'have any of your committee members walked up to Onslow Village on a wet day? If you do so, perhaps we will get our buses back'. Another resident felt that the remaining A&D service 30 was inadequate, with insufficient capacity for the demand. 'I hope the Watch Committee will put the screw on, as the A&D behave as if they owned the town'.

Unfortunately, the Graham Dodge vehicle did not prove particularly successful, being a persistent source of mechanical trouble and spending more time under repair than on the road. Therefore, June 1930 saw the arrival of two more tried and tested Chevrolets with fourteen-seat bus bodywork, registered HX 320/482.

On 28 November 1930, the Board of Aldershot & District was told that a formal Working Agreement was about to be ratified with Arthur Newman, which accorded with the truce brokered in December 1929. The actual document, which still exists, was dated 5 December 1930 and was signed for A&D by director Sidney Garcke. It stipulated that Safeguard would not compete with any A&D service in a large area bordered by Reading, Andover, Winchester, Chichester, Horsham, Dorking and Staines. This agreement and the enactment of the Road Traffic Act 1930 meant that Safeguard's bus services enjoyed a period of stability through the 1930s, which must have been a relief after the turbulent late 1920s.

CONSOLIDATION AND TROUBLES IN THE 1930s

The Westborough service had deviated from the Aldershot Road to serve the residential area of Deerbarn Road and Weston Road. By March 1931 there was pressure from residents to have the buses removed from these narrow streets. A petition was sent to the Town Clerk, who forwarded it to the new South Eastern Traffic Commissioner, who was in the process of taking over bus service licensing from local authorities. The petition cited danger at road junctions (there had already been some accidents involving buses turning), vibrations to houses and the fact that the roads had already been re-surfaced due to high volumes of bus movement. It also stated that those who lived on corners especially had to endure the noise of horns blowing, brake applications, gear changing and pulling away in low gear. There was a maximum walk of 100 yards to the main road, which is where it was suggested that buses should be. On 8 May 1931 a young motor-cyclist from Farncombe was knocked off his machine by a Safeguard bus at the corner of Weston and Deerbarn Roads, bringing forth further protest. Although a counter-petition was organised in support of not changing the route, Safeguard were instructed to remain on the Aldershot Road from June 1931.

In spring 1931 Safeguard made their first applications for road service licenses under the Road Traffic Act 1930. These were to continue stage services from Guildford to Westborough and Guildford Park, excursions and tours from Guildford (North Street) and express services daily in summer from Guildford to Brighton, Worthing, Bognor and Littlehampton. All these applications were granted and continued basically unchanged up to the Second World War, being successfully renewed periodically. Aldershot & District also ran seasonal express services to south coast resorts and, in February 1933, Safeguard successfully opposed A&D in the Traffic Court, preventing the latter from picking up in Guildford and Godalming for Worthing, on their Brighton service.

At times the bus services were so busy that even the larger thirty-two-seat vehicles then employed were carrying in excess of their licensed capacity. This resulted in a summons of Safeguard to the Guildford Borough Bench in late February 1933. PC Kendall had noted fifty-eight people on a bus licensed for thirty-two seats plus five standing, on a Saturday evening. It had been snowing and many people wanted to get home at the same time. Conductor Fred Sheppard asked some passengers

Above left: The original Chevrolet buses were replaced in March 1931 with two twenty-seaters with REAL bodywork on Dennis two-ton lorry chassis. These were far more substantial than the earlier vehicles and construction and design techniques had moved forward considerably. HX 9684 was photographed when brand new, being in the fleet until 1937 when it was sold to a firm in east London. Its twin, HX 9683, is thought not to have been disposed of until late 1942. (*Safeguard Collection*)

Above right: The coach fleet was also modernised in 1931, with this smart Dennis GL, featuring that manufacturer's latest style of radiator. HX 9688 was the last vehicle with bodywork by REAL that Safeguard purchased and was sold in 1936, later being converted to become an ambulance in Woking. (*Safeguard Collection*)

Right: Remaining loyal to locally-produced Dennis products, two Lancets with highly-appointed thirty-two-seat coachwork by Duple (PJ 5158/9) were purchased in spring 1932. Like a number of Safeguard vehicles, these had a dual purpose, being initially used for coach work in summer but they also performed regularly on the bus services. PJ 5159 was not sold (to White Heather of Southsea) until 1949, having been re-bodied by Dennis as a less-luxurious bus in 1939. Seen here in Woodbridge Road on the Westborough service. (*J. F. Higham/Alan Cross*)

The other 1932 Dennis Lancet (PJ 5158) is seen, probably in the mid-1930s, splashing its way along a flooded Woodbridge Road in Guildford. Such conditions never deterred Safeguard from maintaining its obligations to its loyal customers. (*Safeguard Collection*)

to alight, but nobody moved. He was fined £1 and the proprietors £2. The Chairman of the Bench said they would not be so lenient in future.

The Newmans decided to incorporate their business as Safeguard Coaches Ltd, this occurring on 15 March 1933, with an authorised capital of £4,000 in £1 Ordinary shares. The first shareholders were Annie Newman and sons John Henry, Frederick Herbert and Albert Harold. At the first formal meeting of the Directors on 21 June, Annie was named as Chairman and the sons as Directors. Dennis Henry Hart was appointed as Company Secretary. After having a leading role in the business, Arthur

Newman had passed away in December 1932, aged about thirty-six, so his estate was represented in shareholding terms by his widow Kate and by Clarence Charles Moldram, a solicitor and trustee of Arthur's estate, who was also appointed as a Director. Also attending the meeting was John Risdon Amphlett, representing Amphlett & Co. of 231 Strand, London WC2, the company's solicitor. The various licences were to be transferred into the company name from the late Arthur Newman's. Annie Newman was willing to have the Hire Purchase agreement for two new Dennis vehicles in her own name. Prior to the company formation, each of the sons were allocated a specific responsibility: John in charge of the coal merchant business, Fred the mechanical engineering and Bert the administration function. The company was, as stated in the Memorandum of Association, 'to acquire and take over the business of Motor Coach Proprietors, Stage and Express Carriage Operators and Coal Merchants', carried on by those named above. By the time of the setting up of the company, a presence nearer Guildford town centre had been obtained, as an office had been opened at 83 Woodbridge Road, leased from Mr G. Franks.

As early as October 1933, Clarence Moldram had received a letter from Aldershot & District seeking to buy the Safeguard business. They offered £8,000 and although tempting (Safeguard's bank account was overdrawn), the Newmans wanted £12,000. However, they struggled on, although by early 1934 it was noted that the coal merchant activity was not performing well. By the middle of 1935, the cash flow position had reached crisis point. John Amphlett advised the Directors to take a reduction in their own remuneration and to make urgent economies in the running of the business, such as taking over some functions from employees. The Secretary had negotiated a loan without previously discussing it or obtaining authorisation from the Directors and there was £670 missing from the accounts. At the Board meeting on 18 June 1935, Dennis Hart was

Dennis Lancet APD 937 looks very impressive when new, with its comfortable coach seats, curtains, roof-mounted luggage rack and Safeguard insignia aloft at the front. This vehicle was not re-bodied like its twin and had to struggle through the war until scrapped in 1946, still with its original Duple body. (*Safeguard Collection*)

Two further Dennis Lancets arrived in May 1933. APD 936 is believed to be at the outer terminus of the Westborough service, prior to being re-bodied by Dennis in 1940. The conductor's 'Bell Punch' ticket punch is visible, but the ticket rack must be inside the vehicle. (*Safeguard Collection*)

summoned and when asked, was unable to give a satisfactory explanation. He eventually admitted the deficiency and was summarily dismissed – his name being removed from the company's vehicles forthwith.

During the summer of 1935, despite another offer to purchase from A&D for £9,000, the Newmans took stock and re-organised. Bert Newman became Company Secretary, assisted by Percy Albert Spink. A new firm of Auditors was appointed, a Mr Walker had loaned £100 and Clarence Moldram resigned. On a brighter note, Messrs R.E.A.L. of Ealing were to be asked if they could supply a new twenty-seat coach immediately.

On 3 June 1935, Annie Newman resigned as Chairman and announced that Andrew Snuggs Fish from Guildford would be her successor. In October 1935, Fish was prepared to loan Safeguard £200 at 5 per cent interest without security and was appointed as a Director and confirmed as Chairman, being allocated one share. For much of the firm's existence, the Company Secretary of Safeguard has traditionally been the Manager – the latter task in essence passed to somebody outside of the family in

1935 in the person of Percy Spink, who was in post for thirty-one years; he too had a shareholding from February 1936 until 1977.

Financial matters continued to be difficult from 1936 through to the outbreak of war. Despite assistance from Fish and from Annie Newman who had loaned her life savings, in July 1936 there was a loss shown on the balance sheet of £2,000. Traffic receipts had increased, but costs had soared out of proportion, including vehicle maintenance expenses. In summer 1937, significant revenue was lost due to unreliable buses and coaches and a certain mechanic was asked to seek employment elsewhere. Fred and Bert Newman would not agree to drive on bus services to save employee wages and at the heat of the moment at the November 1938 Directors' meeting, Fred suggested that the business be sold. There were no seconders and when Fish suggested that the Bognor express licence be sold to A&D, Amphlett advised against that on principle. Despite the fiscal stringency, money was found to have an electricity supply installed at the garage in 1936.

No doubt becoming the front-line coach on delivery in March 1936, with the streamlined appearance of its Duple bodywork, this is DPH 990, a six-cylinder Dennis Lancet. It had been exhibited the previous autumn at the Commercial Motor Show in London. The Newmans were doubtless very angry when it was compulsorily requisitioned to aid the war effort only four years after its arrival. (*Safeguard Collection*)

The 1930s saw improvements made in bus and coach design and manufacture, with the availability of larger, more luxurious and more robust vehicles. Between 1931 and 1935 the Chevrolets and the Graham Dodge were replaced with new vehicles, predominantly from the local factory of Dennis. In March 1931 came two of that firm's two-ton lorry chassis but fitted with twenty-seat forward control bus bodies by REAL, to be followed by a twenty-seat Dennis GL coach. 1932/3 saw a great step forward, with the arrival of four Dennis Lancet chassis with thirty-two-seat Duple bodies, not only for excursions, express services and private hire, but to bring a touch of comfort to the fortunate folk of Westborough. Following a Dennis Ace coach in 1935, there arrived a luxurious Dennis Lancet 6 cylinder coach in April 1936, after being exhibited at the Commercial Vehicle Show at Olympia the previous year. The engine in this coach got very hot, much to the chagrin of the driver in his cab on warm summer days. In spring 1934, thought was given to obtaining a Public Service Vehicle licence for a large Wolseley car (OU 26) but it was decided that it was not worth the effort.

To release some of the Dennis Lancets from the Westborough service for summer coach duties, two Tilling Stevens/Willowbrook thirty-two-seat buses were acquired from Trent Motor Traction in winter 1936/7; these only remained in use for two years. The first of many Bedford vehicles – a WTB model registered GPF 66 – came in March 1938, to be followed by another (JPB 125) in July 1939. In addition, there were two second hand Dennis vehicles in July 1938 – an example of the Arrow model for coach work and a Lancet for bus work, to replace one of the Tilling Stevens vehicles. Meanwhile, the timber-framed bodies on the first Lancets were already deteriorating. In December 1938, one (PJ 5158) was given a new thirty-two-seat Willowbrook bus body at a cost around £500, while PJ 5159 was similarly re-bodied by Dennis themselves in 1939.

The most significant bus service alteration during the 1930s affected the Guildford Park route. When the renewal of the licence came before the Metropolitan Traffic Commissioner (Guildford had by then been transferred to that area from the South Eastern) in March 1935, Safeguard asked to extend the service to Dennisville (Raymond Crescent). This was to serve the new houses being constructed for Dennis Bros. employees, to start at such a time as the roads were completed and the houses had reached the stage of first occupation. Not surprisingly, A&D made the same request for their service 27. The Commissioner adjourned the applications as he was concerned that buses could present a danger to young children playing in the estate roads and asked the Town Clerk for an opinion. Safeguard also sought the Council's views on when the roads might be ready and whether they would be suitable for the twenty-seat bus proposed to be used. The matter took some time to resolve and Safeguard and A&D did not extend their services beyond The Oval to a bus reversing point at St. Johns Road/Raymond Crescent until 17 June 1936.

In April 1939, Aldershot & District made an offer to purchase Safeguard Coaches for £14,000. However, this was refused by the Newmans who now sought at least £21,000, thus nothing further transpired. In October that year, Frederick Newman passed away; Fred died at a relatively young age from Tuberculosis, apparently through drinking unpasteurised milk from the family cow, as had Frank, another Newman brother. The coal merchant business was still performing poorly and on the advice of the Accountant, it was terminated in 1939 and the Bedford coal lorry was sold that October.

Above: To enable two of the Dennis Lancets to be returned to coaching duties for another season, the winter of 1936/7 saw the acquisition of two elderly Tilling Stevens buses with Willowbrook bodywork, to fill the gap temporarily on the Westborough service. TV 7472 is seen in the livery of its original owner – Unity – although it came to Safeguard via Trent Motor Traction which had acquired the Unity business. It was sold by Safeguard after just a couple of years. (*Safeguard Collection*)

Right: A Safeguard day excursion advertisement which appeared in the *Surrey Advertiser* newspaper on 14 May 1938. The vehicle depicted is DPH 990, the 1936 Dennis Lancet.

SAFEGUARD COACHES LTD.

TOURS ON

		FARE	Depart North St. Old Fire Station
Sunday, (Tomorrow) **May 15**			
BOGNOR REGIS (½ day)		**4/6** Children Half Price	2.15 p.m.
WINDSOR		**3/6** Children 2/-	2.15 p.m.
EVENING TOUR		**2/6** Children 2/-	6.30 p.m.

SPECIAL TOURS TO WHIPSNADE ZOO

	Fare	
WEDNESDAY, MAY 18	**5/-** Children 3/6	10.0 a.m.
SUNDAY, MAY 29		10.15 a.m.

83, WOODBRIDGE ROAD,
Phone **GUILDFORD** 1103

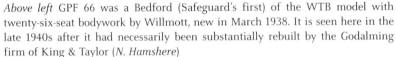

Above left GPF 66 was a Bedford (Safeguard's first) of the WTB model with twenty-six-seat bodywork by Willmott, new in March 1938. It is seen here in the late 1940s after it had necessarily been substantially rebuilt by the Godalming firm of King & Taylor (*N. Hamshere*)

Above right: GY 1198, a Dennis Arrow with thirty-two-seat London Lorries bodywork was acquired in July 1938 from the Motor Transport Co. of London SE14, in whose fleet it is seen. It was accompanied by GY 2221, a Dennis Lancet from the same source. Both vehicles were requisitioned by the War Department in 1940. (*K. Wheal Collection*)

Right: A second Bedford WTB/Willmott twenty-six-seater (JPB 125) arrived new about two months before war was declared in September 1939. It avoided being requisitioned and remained in the fleet until March 1952 when it passed to Mr Murphy of New Malden. (*N. Hamshere*)

WAR AND AUSTERITY

The activities of Safeguard and the lives of its customers on its services and excursions were drastically altered with the declaration of war on 3 September 1939. Due to the fear of night time aerial attack, vehicle headlamps had to be masked and white paint applied to the bodywork to make them more visible to other road users in the 'blackout' conditions. Street lighting was turned off and bus interior lighting had to be greatly reduced, making life very challenging for drivers and conductors. Coastal services and day trips were suspended for the winter and remained so for the duration, while Private Hire virtually ceased. As staff began to be called-up to serve in the Forces, it became necessary to employ lady conductresses, a custom that was to persist for many years afterwards. On Saturdays and during peak hours, the bus services were extremely busy, with Dennis Lancets often requiring duplication by a smaller Dennis or Bedford. At this time there were five buses and five coaches and two of the latter were employed on contracts carrying essential civilian war-workers.

Andrew Fish was appointed Managing Director for a two year period from 1 January 1941, jointly with Bert Newman. Percy Spink continued as Secretary and gained a larger shareholding. The remaining un-allotted 119 shares in the company were vested in Andrew Fish.

Dennis Lancet APD 936 had its Duple rear-entrance coach body replaced at the Dennis factory by a new one with a front entrance and bus seats in 1940, although its twin, APD 937 retained its original body until withdrawn in 1946. War Department staff scoured the country looking to requisition suitable vehicles for use as troop transport. Safeguard lost their two oldest vehicles in this way in 1940 – Dennis Arrow GY 1198 and Dennis Lancet GY 2221. Some replacement was provided by the second-hand acquisition of another Dennis Lancet (DMX 4) but shortly afterwards the Requisitioning Officers called at Ridgemount again, taking not only that coach but also the six-cylinder Lancet of 1936 (DPH 990). Subsequently two more second-hand Lancets were obtained as well as a Bedford WTB, in order to maintain fleet strength. With the use of cars on a private basis virtually non-existent, due to strict petrol rationing, the bus services – especially to Westborough – were extremely busy. Safeguard obtained the necessary Permits from the Ministry of Supply so as to be able to buy two utility Bedford OWB thirty-two-seat buses, fitted with uncomfortable wooden slatted seats: JPK 783 in

Left above: Three of Safeguard's Duple-bodied Dennis Lancets were given new bus bodies between 1938 and 1940 in order to get a few more years use out of the chassis. Representing these is PJ 5159 with locally-produced Dennis bodywork, in this wartime view at the Theatre Royal terminus point of the Westborough service, on the corner of Leapale Road in Guildford. (*Omnibus Society*)

Right above: Also by the Theatre Royal is GY 208, which received the Dennis bus body originally intended for APD 937 in 1943. It had previously been acquired with a Duple coach body from Ridd of London W6 in late 1940, to help replace the vehicles that had been taken for War Department use. (*London Trolleybus Preservation Society*)

Right: Although we can only see the front of Dennis Lancet AOR 76, acquired from Gilder & Blue Motor Services of Bishops Waltham in June 1941, it is the only photograph of it discovered showing it with Safeguard. In the right background there appears one of the prefabricated homes built at Westborough after the war, to relieve the serious local housing shortage. (*Safeguard Collection*)

1942 and JPL 759 in 1944. Dennis Lancet GY 208 purchased in 1940, was able to receive a new Dennis bus body in 1943 – the one originally destined for APD 937, the body on the latter being in the better condition of the two. When GY 208 returned from the Dennis works, its roof was painted grey, theoretically to make it less conspicuous from the air. Guildford had its share of enemy bombing activity, with seventy-four reported incidents with a loss of seven lives between August 1940 and August 1944, when a V1 Rocket (Doodlebug) landed in Aldersey Road.

For reasons connected with potential bombing raids, the number of locations where petrol could be stored was greatly reduced, which meant that a small bus company like Safeguard could no longer use its own tank at Ridgemount. Therefore, the vehicles had to be re-fuelled with 'pool' petrol (usual brand names were abolished) at a garage on the Guildford Bypass. To save fuel, buses had to stay on their designated routes; when one driver took his bus home to Northway at lunch time, he was soon in trouble when it was noticed by a police motorcycle patrolman. As the war progressed, bus operators were obliged to reduce their mileage at off-peak times, to effect further fuel economy. From 4 January 1943 Safeguard withdrew their late evening buses (last departure to Westborough became 9 p.m. and to Dennisville 8.45 p.m.) while all services were withdrawn on Sundays before 1 p.m.

Back in May 1937, Fred Newman had invited John Amphlett to buy 100 of his shares. Amphlett declined, saying that the shares were never intended to be traded on the open market and any dividends should be used as remuneration for those working in the business. However, Andrew Fish died suddenly in summer 1943 and Amphlett agreed to be a Director and was asked to take the chairmanship, due to his proven wisdom and as in-house legal advisor. Shares were then transferred to him, while Andrew Fish's shareholding passed in October 1944 to his son, Charles Andrew Fish, which he held until September 1961.

As the Allies advanced across mainland Europe after D-Day in 1944, the chance of an attack on the UK from a manned aircraft diminished significantly. Thus, it was possible to dispense with grey roofs on buses and 'blackout' restrictions were eased, allowing exterior and interior lighting to be restored to normal strength. Following the end of the war in 1945, it was not possible for bus construction to immediately return to full peace-time standards. However, enhancements were approved for the utility Bedford OWB, giving it a far more attractive appearance than its predecessor and upholstered seating. Safeguard took delivery of two of these buses, each costing £1,127, in 1946 – KPC 658 and KPE 455. Initially they were used as 'coaches', for they were then the best vehicles in the Safeguard fleet. With the easing of petrol rationing (although still fairly stringent for private motoring), the war-weary Guildfordians were extremely eager to go on day trips to the coast, either by licensed Excursion or as a Private Hire. For a while, the beaches were still covered with anti-invasion barbed wire, but people made the best of it. In due course late evening and Sunday morning bus services were restored.

When the coastal scheduled Express services re-started, they too were extremely popular. People were willing to travel long distances on less-comfortable bus seats, such was the demand. On most summer Sundays, the garage at Ridgemount would be empty, with all the coaches and any spare buses away on day trips. With little likelihood of obtaining early delivery of new vehicles (materials were in short supply), Safeguard, like most other operators, had to make do with what they had. Vehicles were sent to local coach works for refurbishment, but the 1938 Bedford WTB (GPF 66) was in such poor condition that it required an almost complete body re-build in July 1947 at King & Taylor Ltd in Godalming. Acquired in August the same year was APX 291, a 1935 Dennis Ace from James Mitchell of Warnham.

The matriarch Annie Newman passed away in March 1946, aged 84. The years immediately following the end of the war were hard, both

Some relief from wartime vehicle shortages was eventually obtained with the delivery of two Bedford OWB/Duple utility buses, which originally had wooden slatted seats. JPK 783 was the first, being delivered in December 1942 after the appropriate Permit had been obtained from the Ministry of Supply. Here it is on 24 October 1943 while working the Dennisville service, which was often operated by the smaller capacity buses. (*J. Gillham*)

KPE 455 was one of two Bedford OB buses with thirty-two-seat Duple bodywork with a somewhat more relaxed specification compared to the original wartime utility design. New in 1946, the pair were subsequently used on coach duties, despite the bus seating, due to the difficulty in obtaining anything more luxurious. However, by the early 1950s they could be used solely on bus services, with this one being blinded for the Northway route, although photographed in Ridgemount. (*N. Hamshere*)

Left: Bert and Ethel Newman photographed on a beach, perhaps on holiday, away from the daily toil of running a seven day a week transport business. (*Newman Family Collection*)

Below: Stalwarts of the Westborough service for around ten years after delivery in summer 1948 as the first post-war new Dennis buses, were MPE 410 and MPF 700. These were Lancet J3 models with thirty-two-seat bodywork by Reading of Portsmouth. MPE 410 is in Farnham Road Bus Station in Guildford, soon to depart for Dennisville. When sold in 1958, it passed to Pioneer Motors (Tudor Williams Bros.) of Laugharne in south-west Wales. (*D. Spencer*)

for people's domestic lives and for businesses like Safeguard. The fleet was depleted and the coaches that had been requisitioned were never returned, although some compensation had been paid. Although business was fairly good – petrol was still rationed – economies were needed and expenditure kept to a minimum, as wages increased significantly in 1947/8. Fare increases approved by the Traffic Commissioner were seen as insufficient. Directors' salaries were reduced and Amphlett even offered to forfeit his entirely from January 1947. The land at Ridgemount on which the garage and cottages stood was owned by the Sussex & Dorking United Brick Co. Ltd and agreement was reached for Safeguard to purchase it in 1949 for £1,900.

The former Mitchell Dennis Ace was bought to supplement the existing Ace (CPL 205) on a new daily bus service running every thirty minutes that was applied for and granted in 1947. One of the utility Bedfords with wooden slatted seats was also used. Like the Westborough service, this started at Leapale Road in Guildford and ran via Woodbridge Road, Woodbridge Hill and Aldershot Road, from where the intention was to diverge so as to serve the housing in Northway, Lincoln Road, Worcester Road and Canterbury Road. Permission to extend was granted in spring 1949, however, it took until 1951 for a proper made-up road link between Aldershot Road and Northway to be provided, so the service initially terminated at Westway, junction with Southway Avenue. The service became popular, requiring a further application in March 1950 to use a twenty-six-seat bus with the driver collecting the fares, becoming known by some as the 'Northway Flyer'.

At the end of the war there was a desperate shortage of affordable or rentable housing in Guildford. Although the Council Houses in Bellfields started to be constructed in January 1946, even more homes were required to deal with the 4,000 applicants on the waiting list. In summer 1946, construction started on 100 pre-fabricated homes ('Prefabs') at

the far end of Westborough, in roads leading off Southway Avenue known as Chapelhouse Road and Park Barn Drive. These were made of aluminium on a factory production line and quickly assembled on site on pre-prepared concrete bases. Compared with much other housing, these offered considerable modernity; fortunate families got a fitted kitchen with electric cooker, washing copper, fridge, fitted wardrobes and a bathroom with hot and cold running water. To serve this new community, Safeguard's Westborough service was extended from Foxburrows Avenue to Park Barn Drive/Chapelhouse in summer 1948. At that time, Safeguard at last took delivery of their first two new post-war buses. These were diesel-engined Dennis Lancet J3s with bus-style bodies by Reading Ltd of Portsmouth, each costing £3,492. Registered MPE 410 and MPF 700, they spent much of their first two summer seasons on coach work, before becoming the main performers on the Westborough service for about a decade.

A bus station was opened in Onslow Street in 1949, although it was not large enough to allow transfer of all bus services from their traditional, congested on-street termini. However, the Aldershot & District/Safeguard joint service to Dennisville did re-locate on 23 June that year, but Safeguard's Westborough and Northway services had to wait until 31 December 1951, when another re-organisation saw the Dennisville service move across to the Farnham Road bus station on the other side of the River Wey.

In early 1950, an additional 9d per gallon was added to fuel tax, costing Safeguard an extra £112 per month, thus spending had to be controlled. Two vehicles arrived, somewhat different to the normal choice of Dennis and Bedford chassis. There was a new Vulcan 6PF with twenty-nine-seat coach bodywork by Dutfield Ltd of Godalming (OPA 883) but also the only double deck bus to be owned. This was HWA 787, a 1943 utility Guy Arab with Weymann fifty-five-seat bodywork, from the municipal

Above: In the late 1940s there was an extremely long lead time to obtain delivery of a coach from a popular manufacturer, due to material shortages and strong demand for new vehicles to replace war-weary examples. Probably in order to obtain something quicker, Safeguard bought OPA 883, a Vulcan 6PF with twenty-nine-seat bodywork by Dutfield Motors Ltd. of Godalming, in March 1950. It was sold in 1956 to Sussex County Council, as it was known then. Seen in Worthing, picking up for the return journey of a coastal express service. (*J. Gillham*)

Left: Something unusual in the Safeguard fleet was a double-decker. HWA 787 was originally no. 487 in the Sheffield municipal fleet, being a Guy Arab II with Weymann bodywork. It came to Guildford after use by Lansdowne Luxury Coaches, an operator and dealer in Leytonstone, Essex. It was used on the Dennisville service for two years from April 1950 (seen here on 10 June that year) and it was to be many years before another double deck vehicle of any description would grace the Safeguard fleet. (*D. Fisk/A. Cross*)

SAFEGUARD COACHES LTI

TIME TABLE

GUILDFORD AND WESTBOROUC

WEEKDAYS

GUILDFORD (*Bus Station*)	6.36	6.48	7.00	7.12	7.24	7.36
DEERBARN ROAD	6.42	6.54	7.06	7.18	7.30	7.42
FOXBURROWS AVENUE	6.48	7.00	7.12	7.24	7.36	7.48
CABELL ROAD TERMINUS	6.54	7.06	7.18	7.30	7.42	7.54

AND EVERY TWELVE MINUTES UNTIL 10.36 P.M.

CABELL ROAD TERMINUS	6.30	6.42	6.54	7.06	7.18	7.30
FOXBURROWS AVENUE	6.36	6.48	7.00	7.12	7.24	7.36
WOODBRIDGE HILL	6.42	6.54	7.06	7.18	7.30	7.42
GUILDFORD (*Bus Station*)	6.48	7.00	7.12	7.24	7.36	7.48

AND EVERY TWELVE MINUTES UNTIL 10.30 P.M.

SUNDAYS

GUILDFORD (*Bus Station*)	10.00	10.20	10.40	Then every
DEERBARN ROAD	10.06	10.26	10.46	20 minutes
FOXBURROWS AVENUE	10.13	10.33	10.53	until 10.20
CABELL ROAD TERMINUS	10.20	10.40	11.00	

CABELL ROAD TERMINUS	10.00	10.20	10.40	Then every
FOXBURROWS AVENUE	10.06	10.26	10.46	20 minutes
WOODBRIDGE HILL	10.13	10.33	10.53	until 10.20
GUILDFORD (*Bus Station*)	10.20	10.40	11.00	

Weekday Service to operate on Sundays from 12.54 p.m. on 1st Sunda in May to last Sunday in September.

8.30 a.m. ex Cabell Road Terminus on Whit Sunday and every Sunday until last Sunday in September.

Boxing Day and Good Friday same as Sunday. Easter Monday Whi Monday and August Bank Holiday, first departure ex Guildford 8.00 a.m ex Cabell Road Terminus 8.06 a.m. then as on weekdays.

Above: Late 1950s timetable.

The first of several second-hand coach acquisitions in the 1950s, was EDL 445, a Bedford OB with ubiquitous Duple Vista twenty-nine-seat bodywork, acquired from Moss Motors of Sandown, Isle of Wight. Coach-type vehicles were often used on the bus services at this time and this example was in Onslow Street bus station in Guildford, soon to depart on the Northway service. (*J. Boylett/sct61*)

Another Bedford OB was MMY 696, acquired in January 1951 having been previously owned by Hall's Coaches of Hillingdon, Middlesex, seen outside the depot at Ridgemount. (*N. Hamshere*)

SAFEGUARD COACHES LTD.

TIME TABLE

GUILDFORD AND DENNISVILLE
Via Guildford Park

WEEKDAYS

		a m	a m	a m	a m	a m	a m	a m			mins.	p m			
Guildford, Farnham Rd., Bus Stn.	dep.	7 20	7 40	8 10	8 30	8 50	9 15	9 45	then	15 45	past	10 15	...	...	...
Guildford, Station Approach	,,	7 22	7 42	8 12	8 32	8 52	9 17	9 47	every	17 47	each	10 17	...	...	...
Guildford, Park Oval	,,	7 26	7 46	8 16	8 36	8 56	9 21	9 51	30 mins.	21 51	hour	10 21	...	...	...
Dennisville, Raymond Crescent	arr.	7 28	7 48	8 18	8 38	8 58	9 23	9 53	at	23 53	until	10 23	...	...	...

		a m	a m	a m	a m	a m	a m	a m			mins.	p m			
Dennisville, Raymond Crescent	dep.	7 10	7 30	7 50	8 20	8 40	9 0	9 30	then	0 30	past	10 0	...	...	...
Guildford, Park Oval	,,	7 12	7 32	7 52	8 22	8 42	9 2	9 32	every	2 32	each	10 2	...	...	...
Guildford, Station Approach	,,	7 16	7 36	7 56	8 26	8 46	9 6	9 36	30 mins.	6 36	hour	10 6	...	...	...
Guildford, Farnham Rd. Bus Stn.	arr.	7 18	7 38	7 58	8 28	8 48	9 8	9 38	at	8 38	until	10 8	...	...	...

SUNDAYS

		a m	a m	a m	a m	p m	p m	p m	p m	p m	p m	p m	p m	p m			mins.
Guildford, Farnham Rd. Bus Stn.	dep.	1045	1115	1145	1215	1 45	2 15	2 45	3 15	3 45	4 15	4 45	5 45	6 15	then	15 45	past
Guildford, Station Approach	,,	1047	1117	1147	1217	1 47	2 17	2 47	3 17	3 47	4 17	4 47	5 47	6 17	every	17 47	each
Guildford, Park Oval	,,	1051	1121	1151	1221	1 51	2 21	2 51	3 21	3 51	4 21	4 51	5 51	6 21	30 mins.	21 51	hour
Dennisville, Raymond Crescent	arr.	1053	1123	1153	1223	1 53	2 23	2 53	3 23	3 53	4 23	4 53	5 53	6 23	at	23 53	until

		a m	a m	noon	p m	p m	p m	p m	p m	p m	p m	p m	p m			mins.
Dennisville, Raymond Crescent	dep.	1030	11 0	1130	12 0	1230	2 0	2 30	3 0	3 30	4 0	4 30	5 0	5 30	then	0 30	past
Guildford, Park Oval	,,	1032	11 2	1132	12 2	1232	2 2	2 32	3 2	3 32	4 2	4 32	5 2	5 32	every	2 32	each
Guildford, Station Approach	,,	1036	11 6	1136	12 6	1236	6 2	2 36	3 6	3 36	4 6	4 36	5 6	5 36	30 mins.	6 36	hour
Guildford, Farnham Rd. Bus Stn.	arr.	1038	11 8	1138	12 8	1238	8 2	2 38	3 8	3 38	4 8	4 38	5 8	5 38	at	8 38	until

Above left: The first of three second hand Dennis Lancet J3 coaches was FHO 769, with full half-cab bodywork by Wadhams of Waterlooville, previously owned by Hutfields of Gosport, Hants and in the Safeguard fleet for just under a year from December 1951. (*N. Hamshere*)

Below left: Another second hand Dennis Lancet J3 was JTU 97, with Yeates bodywork, used for a couple of seasons almost exclusively for excursions and private hire. (*N. Hamshere*)

Above left: Replacing the Guy Arab double-decker was Dennis Lancet J3 ENT 581, from the large fleet of Salopia Coaches of Whitchurch, Shropshire. This was photographed at the St John's Road/Raymond Crescent terminus point of the Dennisville service. (*N. Hamshere*)

Above right: Also emanating from Salopia Coaches, was FAW 532, another Bedford OB/Duple Vista, owned from November 1952 and sold to Odiham Motor Services in October 1960. (*Safeguard Collection*)

Right: A portrait of Bernard Newman, probably taken in the 1950s. (*Newman Family Collection*)

Sheffield fleet. However, for a couple of months in 1949 it was used by dealer and operator Lansdowne Luxury Coaches of Leytonstone in Essex, on contracts carrying building workers to new London County Council housing sites, before being sold to Safeguard for £750. Since the end of the war, loadings on the Dennisville service had increased and a double-decker seemed an appropriate solution.

Those collecting the bus from Essex first had to find it, as it was out on a contract working. It seems that Lansdowne had fitted wooden slatted seats in place of the Sheffield upholstered ones (perhaps considered more durable for transporting grubby builders!) so these were replaced on arrival at Guildford with seats from a Bedford OB bus on the upper deck and seats from one of the pre-war Dennis Lancet buses on the lower deck. However, the 'decker was too tall to access the garage at Ridgemount, making maintenance difficult. After a couple of years, patronage of the Dennisville service had somewhat decreased so the Guy was sold in spring 1952, eventually ending up as a Showman's vehicle. On the subject of maintenance, a shed at Ridgemount was demolished in 1952 and replaced with a workshop building just large enough for one vehicle.

THE HEYDAY OF THE BUS INDUSTRY

There was felt to be a need for better coaches, if affordable, as receipts from excursions and express services were down by £282 in 1950, due to competition from A&D which had new vehicles. The 1950s were characterised by the periodic purchase by Safeguard of new buses and good quality second-hand coaches, the latter mainly about three years old at the time. The reason for this was that regular Service buses had heavy daily usage and high mileage, whereas coach use was predominantly seasonal, although they too were also used on the bus services at times. Four Bedford OB and three Dennis Lancet coaches appeared between 1951 and 1954, before the larger Bedford SB model, with a capacity varying between thirty-three and forty-one, became the favoured choice. By the end of 1954, all the pre-war and wartime vehicles had been sold, while in that year Safeguard took advantage of the new maximum permitted length for a bus of thirty feet, by taking delivery of two Bedford SB/Duple Midland thirty-nine-seat buses – UPK 615 and VPJ 750. In October 1955 a Bedford SB coach formerly owned by Coliseum of Southampton (KCG 974) arrived in a green, cream and fawn/grey livery. The green was re-sprayed red, thus introducing Safeguard's new coach livery to replace the previous red, cream and maroon. The bus livery was standardised on red and cream. Four more Coliseum Bedfords were subsequently purchased, no doubt because they came from a good source and could be easily re-liveried.

Meanwhile, a new trio of front-line buses for the Westborough service was required, enabling the last of the Dennis Lancets to be eventually replaced. As Dennis did not have a tried and tested under-floor-engine single deck chassis readily available, Safeguard turned to the popular AEC Reliance. Two forty-four-seaters with attractive Burlingham bodywork arrived in 1956 (registered co-incidentally as 200 APB and 200 BPG) while a third, also with Burlingham body but to a revised style, registered 197 DPK, came in October 1957.

In the mid-1950s, Bert Newman's two sons, Bernard Frank and Kenneth Harold became shareholders, having been Working Directors to support their father since December 1954 and December 1956 respectively, being the third generation of the family to have an active role in the business. It was Bern and Ken who were to drive the firm forward for the next forty years. On a day to day basis, most of their time was spent in the workshop,

Above left: This is Safeguard's first Bedford SB (GDW 981) which had a thirty-three-seat Duple body. It came from Alpha Coaches of Brighton in March 1954 and was photographed in Guildford's Onslow Street bus station. (*J. Boylett/sct61*)

Above right: 1954 saw the introduction of the first thirty feet long buses in the form of two Bedford SBOs (with diesel engines) and thirty-nine-seat bodywork by Duple Midland. VPJ 750 purports to be acting as a Relief bus – the other was UPK 615, which became the first of several Safeguard vehicles to be sold to H. R. & V. Gunn (Safeway Services) of South Petherton, Somerset. (*K. Wheal Collection*)

maintaining the vehicles, as routine administration matters were dealt with by the Manager.

During the war, Bern had worked on munitions production at the nearby Dennis factory, where he met his future wife Catherine – known to all as Kit. After National Service in the RAF, he joined the family business and took a leading role in vehicle body repairs. Bern and Kit had lived in Ludlow Road, a stone's throw from the bus garage and in due course acquired land from Safeguard in Ridgemount to have a bungalow built. Their son Graham John was born in July 1951.

Ken first knew his future wife Gill from the age of ten and started going out with her when he was sixteen. They married in 1949 after which Ken had to do his National Service, also in the RAF. He was stationed at various places including Lyneham and while he was away, Gill stayed with Bert Newman and his wife, who were then living at Ash Grove, having previously been at Agraria Road. On release from the air force, Ken was apprenticed to Barnes, a local garage, for five years, gaining comprehensive motor engineering skills, before joining Safeguard. He was also very clever at making things out of wood, such as toys for the children. Their son, David Kenneth, arrived in August 1952. In the 1950s and later, Ken was working long hours to keep the fleet on the road, only having Sunday afternoon off, unless called out for a breakdown. He was in the garage by 6 a.m. each morning, making sure the vehicles were ready for the road. Conditions at the old workshop were extremely harsh – no heating of any sort, no doors except for a heavy canvas curtain and no inspection pit or hoist; on one occasion, Ken came very close to having frostbite. He would cycle to work, not owning a car of his own until the mid 1950s. Ken and Gill had a house built in Queen Eleanor's Road in Onslow Village, near the A3 and later moved to Levylsdene, on the Merrow side of Guildford. Of the era just described, Gill Newman said 'they were good days, but hard – but we enjoyed it – you had to have a good sense of humour'.

Guildford Council was building more conventional housing in Westborough, as green fields gave way to bricks and mortar. From 10 November 1957, the Westborough bus service was extended from Chapelhouse to a point along the new Cabell Road and in April 1959 beyond to the Youth Centre. By then the service interval on the Westborough route had been slightly widened from every ten minutes to every twelve minutes, although on Sundays it remained at every twenty minutes. In terms of company premises, the old timber and corrugated iron garage at Ridgemount was demolished in 1957 and replaced by an extended and more robust building, erected alongside the 1952 workshop. Meanwhile, the town centre office had moved by 1957 from Woodbridge Road to more convenient shop premises in Sutton Buildings in Onslow Street, near to the old cattle market. Safeguard could there display details of their Express Services and Excursions, encouraging the public to call in and book a seat. People would actually queue there and at later offices, in January, to book their excursions and tickets to the coast on the express services, as soon as the new brochure was released.

Between 1959 and 1961, further new Bedford buses with Duple Midland bodywork were acquired – an SB1 registered 250 LPB and two Leyland-engined SB8s, registered 630 SPH and 699 VPL. In terms of coaches, previous policy was reversed, whereby most were now bought new, with only the occasional second-hand purchase. Most were diesel-engined Bedford SB variants with forty-one-seat Duple or Plaxton bodywork. In January 1961, Bedford bus UPK 615 was sold to Herbert & Veronica Gunn's Safeway Services of South Petherton in Somerset. Herbert Gunn always looked for well-maintained second-hand purchases and as Safeguard's and Safeway's livery was similar, all he had to do was eventually paint the roof maroon. The following year he purchased Safeguard's AEC Reliance 200 APB, which will feature again later in this story.

Above: The earliest vehicle for which a colour image has been sourced, is 200 APB, one of a pair of forty-four-seat Burlingham-bodied AEC Reliance buses delivered in 1956. AEC was to replace Dennis as the preferred supplier of heavyweight buses to Safeguard. It shows the yard at Ridgemount Garage in the days before it was properly surfaced and before the demolition of Nos 1/3 Ridgemount. This bus was another to be sold to Herbert and Veronica Gunn and will fortuitously reappear later in this story. (*K. Wheal*)

Copy of account from E.J.Baker & Co. in respect of Bus 200 BPG.

```
   To supplying one new A.E.C. Reliance Chassis fitted Burlingham
44 str Bus body as detailed below.         2357  -  -
                          less discount      250  -  -
                                            2107  -  -

    To supplying and fitting.
One new 44 seater fixed roof single decked
omnibus body of all metal construction
to our B.E.design 30' long and 8' wide,
fitted with one fog lamp, standard partitions
behind driver, special type seats giving a
wider gangway,and which seats are normally
fitted to a vehicle 7'6" wide, seats upholstered
in Firths red No.214 moquette and red No.2;6 vynide,
with lite iron treads in gangway and between seats
full length handrail above o/s gangway, 2 conductor
boxes and mounted on the above chassis and to
official contract No.1858 dated 27/6/56.   2198  10  -
Fitting Jack knife doors with teleflex
operation in place of manually operated doors  28 10  -
   Delivery charges                           15  -  -
Certificate of Fitness                         5  -  -
                                            _____
                                            4354  -  -

Allowance on Dennis and Vulcan
Coaches ENT 581 and OPA 883                 1000  -  -
                                            _____
                                           £3354  -  -

Receipt with B.M.T.Contracts Ltd.,
```

Above: The account from the supplying dealer – E. J. Baker & Co. – for 200 BPG, the other 1956 AEC Reliance/Burlingham bus.

Left: The second of five good quality Bedford SBs sourced by E. J. Baker from the Southampton-based fleet of Coliseum Coaches, was MHO 627 – a Bedford SBG with Duple Vega thirty-eight-seat bodywork. These came in a green, cream and fawn/grey livery. By repainting the green to red, Safeguard established a new coach livery. (*J. Boylett/sct61*)

Above left: Ken and Gill Newman with their son David and daughter Therese. Both children are currently Directors of Safeguard Coaches Ltd. (*Newman Family Collection*)

Above right: Bert Newman's wife Ethel, with grandsons David and Graham. (*Newman Family Collection*)

Above left: To complete the trio of frontline buses for the Westborough service, AEC Reliance 197 DPK was purchased new in October 1957. Its forty-five-seat Burlingham body was to a revised style from that on the earlier Reliance buses. In the background are some of the Westborough prefabs as well as what looks like a wartime 'Anderson' air raid shelter. (*K. Wheal Collection*)

Above right: Lasting with Safeguard for three years from May 1958 was MXL 746, another Bedford SB/Duple, previously owned by Phillips of Cinderford, Gloucestershire. It appears to be on a private hire job at Wembley, at a spot which appears in many other contemporary photographs taken of coaches. (*Author's Collection*)

Below left: Another former Coliseum vehicle was PAA 207, a 1956 Bedford SBG with Duple's classic revised Vega body, featuring forty-one seats and a butterfly-shaped radiator grille. The window bill says that it was on hire to Ben Stanley Ltd, another well-known Surrey coach operator, based in Hersham near Walton on Thames. (*K. Wheal Collection*)

Above: Typical of the Bedford buses employed on the Northway service was 250 LPB, a Bedford SB1 diesel with thirty-five-seat Duple Midland body, new in 1959. Photographed on 1 June 1963, it is turning right from Aldershot Road into Northway on a section of road constructed in 1951, despite a licence being obtained for the planned service in 1949. (*K. Wheal Collection*)

Below: The final former Coliseum coach to enter the fleet was RHO 553, in October 1959, being another Bedford SBG/Duple Vega. It shows off the coach livery adopted in the 1950s and behind it in Ridgemount is VCE 520, a diesel-engined Bedford SB. (*K. Wheal*)

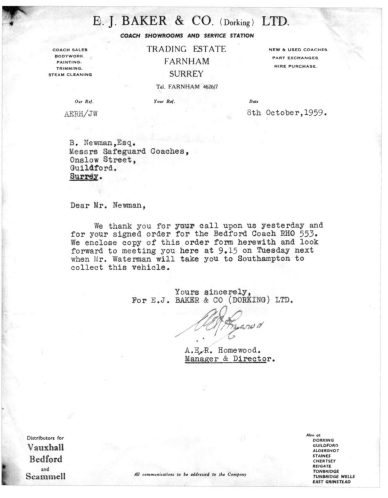

Interestingly, some correspondence between dealer E. J. Baker & Co. and Bert Newman, concerning RHO 553, has survived to be reproduced here.

Above left: Another Wembley view features 144 PPH (with RHO 553 behind), the last petrol-engined Bedford coach to be acquired. It was also the first of Safeguard's vehicles with Plaxton bodywork, being a forty-one-seater of their Embassy model. (*K. Wheal Collection*)

Above right: Further buses arrived in 1961 in the form of two Bedford SB8/Duple Midland forty-one-seaters, with Leyland diesel engines. The first was 630 SPH, photographed soon after delivery. When sold in 1966, it passed to Banstead Coaches for their Chipstead Valley to Banstead service and in 1972 it was purchased by Tony McCann of Forest Green for his service thence to Guildford which he had recently started after the collapse of North Downs Rural Transport. (*Safeguard Collection*)

John Newman, who had lost an eye and became blind after an accident while gardening and had been very deaf for years which affected his speech, died in November 1960 and in due course his shareholding passed to his widow, Grace, until her death in June 1971.

In October 1962, another AEC Reliance/Willowbrook bus (5389 PL) was delivered, before the maximum permitted length for a public service vehicle was increased to thirty-six feet. To take advantage of this, the first buses of such length in the area were three AEC Reliance/Willowbrook buses with fifty-three seats which arrived in 1963/4 (1637 PF, APA 46B and EPH 189B), while the last vehicle with a petrol engine – Bedford SB3/Plaxton coach 144 PPH, was sold in January 1963. The first thirty-six foot coach was HPB 951C, a Bedford VAL14 with fifty-two-seat Plaxton bodywork in March 1965. The VAL chassis had smaller than usual wheels, with twin axles at the front.

At Ridgemount, by 1962 the workshop built in 1952 was already very inadequate, so the main garage building was extended to encompass a workshop area under one roof and the old workshop was demolished. This was a great improvement over the previous somewhat primitive facilities, where David and Gill Newman recall Bert and Ken lying in mud to work underneath coaches; with such conditions it is tribute to their skills that vehicles were always clean and well-maintained. A heating system was installed, previous to which it was necessary for Bern Newman to use the only source of warmth – a paraffin heater – to make bodywork filler set in the winter. Safeguard's mechanics could then show their versatile skills in undertaking all forms of maintenance and refurbishing, including rebuilding gearboxes and re-lining engines.

Above left: The second Bedford SB1/Plaxton Embassy coach was 310 TPK from 1961. It is standing near the then Safeguard office at Sutton Buildings in Onslow Street, Guildford. (*K. Wheal Collection*)

Above right: This photograph depicts a fine view of Bedford SB1/Plaxton Embassy 739 UPF on delivery in July 1961. It remained in the fleet for just over four years, then the average for a Bedford coach with Safeguard. (*Safeguard Collection*)

Below left: Sourced through a dealer was VCE 520, a Bedford SBI with Duple Super Vega bodywork. It was previously owned by Harveys of Cambridge, left the fleet in January 1964 but returned in March 1967 from E. J. Baker's operational fleet for one more summer season, to cope with extra demand for coaches. (*Author's Collection*)

Below right: The first Bedford SB model with the updated Bedford diesel engine was this SB5 with Duple Super Vega bodywork and registered 729 XPF in April 1962. Its next owner was Hutchinson of London SE25. (*Safeguard Collection*)

The construction of the new Guildford Cathedral of the Holy Spirit on Stag Hill had started as far back as 1936 but all work stopped for the duration of the war. Many of the bricks were actually produced from the brickfield adjacent to Ridgemount, which was in use until the 1950s. Work resumed in 1948 but had virtually stopped again six years later through lack of funding. Then, the Mayor of Guildford, Leslie Codd, told the Clergy that the unfinished building was 'a discredit to Guildford. Either sell it or finish it'. He started a fund and suggested that people subscribed to the cost of bricks at 2s 6d each. This raised £56,000 and,

with other funding, enabled consecration by 1963. To cater for visitors, some journeys on Safeguard's Dennisville service, as well as some of those operated by Aldershot & District on their service 27, were extended up to the building from 27 May 1963. Each company ran as far as Dennisville every thirty minutes, resulting in an integrated four buses per hour.

In the early 1960s, David Newman and his cousin Graham, as young lads, regarded the bus garage and the adjoining land as their playground, especially during school holidays. They spent much time scavenging for old materials so they could make trolleys and bikes and playing with

Above left: 5389 PL was an AEC Reliance bus with attractive Willowbrook forty-five-seat bodywork, replacing 200 APB in autumn 1962, which then departed for Somerset. (*Safeguard Collection*)

Above right: The next Bedford SB5, 1920 PJ delivered in March 1963, carried Duple's new forty-one-seat Bella Vega bodywork. (*Safeguard Collection*)

the old ticket racks and punches, which by then had been replaced by Setright and Ultimate roll ticket machines. In his early teens, David would earn pocket money by assisting with jobs around the yard and recalls that on Saturday mornings he would help his grandfather count cash at the Sutton Buildings office. On Sunday mornings he would wash and sweep out vehicles. In those days, lots of people smoked in the buses and coaches, so this required an annual internal deep-cleaning task. The interior surfaces were coated in brown nicotine stain and tar and much elbow grease was expended by scrubbing with neat Teepol to try and get it off.

In 1965, the Safeguard office had moved from Sutton Buildings to a purpose-built but temporary building in Friary Square, near the footbridge across the river that linked the Onslow Street and Farnham Road bus stations. By 1969 it had to be moved to a converted caravan obtained from Bill McAllister at Gomshall, until the Borough Council completed new bus enquiry offices at the rear of the Onslow Street bus station in early 1972.

Above right: The first bus thirty-six-feet long, and the first Safeguard AEC Reliance with air rather than vacuum brakes, was 1637 PF in September 1963. Its Willowbrook bodywork contained fifty-three seats, with extra capacity being welcomed for the busy Westborough service. (*G. Button Collection*)

Below right: Since the last Bedford OB had left the fleet in October 1960, there had been no coach of twenty-nine-seat capacity for smaller groups of customers. This was remedied three years later with the acquisition of 119 GBM, a Bedford VAS1 with Duple Bella Vista body, previously owned by Cook's Coaches of Biggleswade. (*Safeguard Collection*)

Above left: The second fifty-three-seat AEC Reliance was APA 46B in December 1963. It is seen here turning from the bus station into Onslow Street. Both 1637 PF and APA 46B went northwards when they left Guildford, to the eclectic fleet of Barton Transport of Chilwell in Nottinghamshire. Today, this street scene is completely changed, with part of the Friary Shopping centre replacing the Pickfords building. (*B. Jenkins/ Online Transport Archive*)

Above right: The final member of the original trio of 'big Reliances' was EPH 189B, which departed for Red Rover Omnibus of Aylesbury, in March 1971. Its location here is self-apparent. (*The Bus Gallery*)

Left: A superb depiction of the first thirty-six-foot coach – HPB 951C. This was a Bedford VAL14 with fifty-two-seat Plaxton Panorama coachwork, dating from March 1965. Its smaller than usual wheels, twin steerable front axles, huge windows and inward pivoting entrance door were somewhat revolutionary at the time. Some drivers called them 'Chinese Sixes' or 'Six Leggers'. (*M. King Collection*)

COACHING EXPANSION AND FLOODING

Another long-established Guildford coach operator was Cooke's Coaches of Stoughton. John Cooke's original garage premises were in Barrack Road, with a grocery shop next door. As the business grew, a move was made to larger premises at Elmbank, 260 Worplesdon Road and on 20 June 1935 it was incorporated as Cooke's Coaches (Stoughton) Ltd. Bus services were not operated, except for a Friday round trip from Blackheath into Guildford for a short time after the acquisition of Rackliffe's Coaches in February 1955. The main business was Private Hire, day excursions and extended holiday tours, as well as Works Contracts. The latter included a number to Vokes factory at Henley Park near Normandy, which had originated during the war. Additional Excursion licences had been obtained by purchase from Cartland & Baker, in 1934 and from H. Rackliffe in 1955. At the start of 1966 the Cookes decided to dispose of their business and discussions were held with Safeguard, with the takeover occurring on 14 March of that year. This involved the transfer of excursion and tour licences, an Express service to the Kent coast, four drivers and five relatively modern Bedford coaches, but not the premises or the Works Contracts, for a consideration of £19,370. For the first season the acquired coaches remained in Cooke's blue and yellow livery, but sign-writing was altered.

Officially from 1 April 1967, William (Bill) Alfred Clifton, who had started working for Safeguard in 1936, was appointed Company Secretary, in place of Percy Spink who retired. Bill was supported in commercial matters from 1969 by Gordon Button, who was appointed as Traffic Manager. Although hailing from Guildford, Gordon had latterly run his own small coach business at Brackley in Northants, which traded under the name of Borderline. The firm continued with some contract work after Gordon moved south, although operations ceased in 1970 when his Bedford SB8/Duple coach 266 BLB was transferred to Safeguard for one season, continuing to carry its Borderline yellow and cream livery.

The sudden increase in the number of coaches in the mid-1960s meant that more space was needed. The adjoining semi-detached cottages, including No. 1 Ridgemount, at one time occupied by Henry and Annie Newman, were demolished so the yard could be enlarged with additional hard-standing. By 1968, these cottages were noted as being in very poor condition, with only one occupied. Safeguard purchased back from Bern

Above left: Of the five coaches acquired with the Cooke's Coaches business of Guildford in March 1966, 644 HAA was the smallest, being a Bedford J2SZ2 with Plaxton eighteen-seat bodywork. In Cooke's blue and yellow livery, it stands in that operator's premises in Worplesdon Road, Stoughton. (*Safeguard Collection*)

Above right: This Bedford VAS1 with twenty-nine-seat Plaxton bodywork incorporating some of the features found on their larger models, also came from Cooke's. The acquisitions spent a relatively short time with Safeguard and for the first summer season they remained in Cooke's colours, with amended sign-writing. The racecourse location could be Epsom or perhaps Goodwood. (*K. Wheal Collection*)

Left: Bedford VAM14/Duple Midland LPB 238D replaced Bedford SB8 630 SPH in spring 1966. It is at stand five in Guildford's Farnham Road bus station which was shared by Safeguard and Aldershot & District service 27 to Dennisville. Its next owner was Newman of Slough (no relation). (*Author's Collection*)

Further spring 1966 deliveries were a pair of Bedford VAM5 coaches with forty-five-seat Plaxton Panorama bodywork. They both left the fleet in the early 1970s. (*Safeguard Collection*)

In May 1967 there arrived another twenty-nine-seat coach – a Bedford VAS5 with Duple Vista bodywork, registered OPF 345E. Duple had recycled the Vista name, having used it for one of the all-time classic combinations of Duple coachwork on the Bedford OB chassis. (*PM Photography*)

Newman the lower portion of his garden at 7 Ridgemount for a further garage extension in 1970. The purchase of the Cooke's licences meant that the excursion and tour programme had been expanded, with a selection of inclusive holiday trips ranging from weekend breaks to full weeks.

The second half of the 1960s saw regular fleet replacement, so that the age profile remained low. There were thirteen new Bedfords with Duple or Plaxton bodywork, with all except one being coaches. These were mainly of the VAM forty-five-seat or VAL fifty-two-seat type.

Torrential rain over the weekend of 14–15 September 1968 resulted in widespread and serious flooding across much of Surrey. With the River Wey running through the middle of it, Guildford town centre was badly affected with water up to six feet deep in places. The flood water reached a peak on Monday, 16 September, with 3,000 people evacuated from their homes and shoppers and sightseers were almost cut off as a sudden rush of water headed in the direction of the two bus stations, which were already flooded. Millbrook, Onslow Street and the bottom of the High Street

Above left: In the late 1960s, Bert Newman (seated front right) displays his trophies won through his membership of Guildford Sea Fishing Association. Standing left to right are Ken, Kit, Gill and Bern Newman. (*Ludi Photographers/Newman Family Collection*)

Above right: Plaxton's forty-one-seat bodywork modelled on the larger Panorama models is fitted to this Bedford SB5 from December 1967, looking very smart in the fawn, cream and red coach livery. (*M. King Collection*)

Above left: Safeguard had a few coaches with Duple's Viceroy bodywork. UPD 381F was a forty-five-seat example on a Bedford VAM70 chassis. Sold in April 1973, it passed to Bexleyheath Transport (Margo's). (*T. W. Knowles*)

Above right: Bedford replaced the VAL14 model with the VAL70, but retaining some of the same features. Plaxton had also replaced the Panorama body with the Panorama Elite, of which Safeguard's first was WPF 872G. The venue is a bus rally in May 1970, perhaps at Stratford-Upon-Avon. (*M. Bennett*)

Right: WPK 365G (and twin WPK 366G) were contemporary deliveries to WPF 872G, but were forty-five-seat Panorama Elite examples, on a Bedford VAM70 chassis. (*Safeguard Collection*)

resembled a lake, but buses continued running by ploughing through the waters as best they could and a temporary terminus point had to be used for several days at St Saviour's Church. The junction of Guildford Park Road, Madrid Road and Ridgemount is at a low point, with at that time an open stream in the vicinity; two feet of flood water flowed through Tubbs' hardware shop and sub post office on the corner, although the Safeguard premises just behind are at a higher level and were unaffected. Former Safeguard driver Brian Williams remembers that bus crews had to be ferried by tractor and trailer from Farnham Road Rail Bridge in order to reach their vehicles. They carried on regardless, even with water coming up the steps of the bus. Bert Newman, who was overseeing things on the spot, gave instruction to just keep going, ignore the timetable, fill up with passengers and get people home. This went on for two or three days, earning the gratitude of the loyal customers – no more than one had come to expect from Safeguard. As a reward for the crews, Bert organised free beer and trays of sandwiches in the Prince of Wales pub, for when they had finished their shifts – 'we felt like Royalty', said Brian.

One of Gordon Button's first tasks on his arrival in 1969 was to investigate the possibility of Safeguard acquiring a base at Cranleigh. Negotiations were opened with an established local operator, but these did not prove fruitful as the asked-for price was deemed too high and a request to inspect the balance sheet was politely refused, thus the acquisition of that firm was unable to be pursued.

An extract of the Guildford town plan from a London Transport local timetable booklet dating from the late 1960s, showing the Safeguard bus routes as they were at that time. The depot on the corner of Madrid Road and Ridgemount can be located on the Dennisville service.

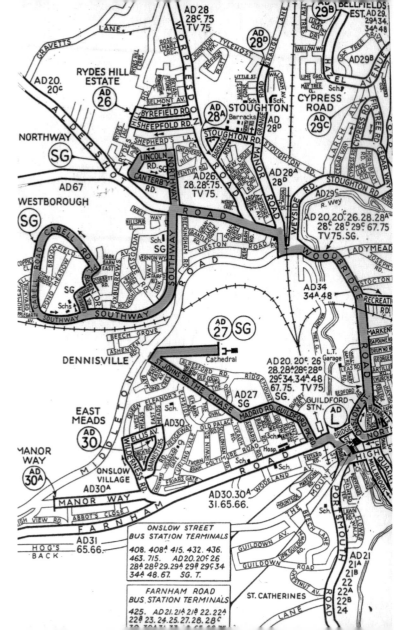

NEW BUSINESS OPPORTUNITIES

The first year of the new decade saw Safeguard's best profits since the company was formed. The early 1970s saw a flurry of bus service developments. First was the extension of some journeys from Dennisville to the new University of Surrey campus from 16 February 1970, although Safeguard's Sunday journeys on this route ceased from 3 July 1971, being then solely provided by A&D on an hourly basis. By the autumn of 1971, Tillingbourne Valley Services Ltd was in various difficulties and found it necessary to reduce operations. This included the withdrawal after 16 October of their Guildford local service 451 to London Road Station, St Luke's Hospital and on up Warren Road to One Tree Corner, which they had run since December 1929. This created a difficulty for bus users in this hilly area of the town. Safeguard came to the rescue by introducing a limited replacement from 25 October, for a trial period of ten weeks. For shoppers there were three round trips Mondays to Fridays and two on Saturdays, while an additional afternoon trip on Tuesdays and Fridays and an evening one on Wednesdays and Fridays were aimed at hospital visitors. The timetable leaflet contained the warning that 'the continuance of this service will depend ENTIRELY on the use made of

same and it must be stressed that loading records will be used to ascertain to what extent the services are truly required. Any lack of demand will incur termination of some or all journeys'. Any concerns that Safeguard had were manifest on 18 December 1971 when they withdrew the service, although part of the route up Warren Road saw buses again in 1973 when Blue Saloon Coaches started their Boxgrove Park service.

Commencement of construction work for a new Guildford town centre gyratory road scheme occurred from spring 1971. On 24 April, two temporary additional bus terminal points were introduced; on-street stops in Millbrook and Commercial Road, although this did not affect Safeguard's services. The footbridge between the Farnham Road and Onslow Street bus stations was closed and later removed, to be replaced by a new road/pedestrian bridge across the River Wey, which for some time was only available for use by people on foot. From July 1972, what was left of Onslow Street bus station was closed, at which point Safeguard's Park Barn and Northway services ran from Farnham Road bus station, while the Dennisville service, along with Alder Valley's services which left town over the Farnham Road railway bridge, were moved to stops

Above left: UAA 751H was one of the pair of Bedford VAM70/Willowbrook forty-five-seat buses purchased in November 1969, the first service buses used by Safeguard that qualified for the government's New Bus Grant. Lacking in capacity and stamina for arduous use on the Park Barn service, they were more acceptable for the quieter Northway and Dennisville routes. (*The Bus Gallery*)

Above right: A new addition to the smaller coaches in late 1969 was UAA 754H, a Bedford VAS5 with Duple Vista 25 bodywork. In late 1973 it stands outside the garage, soon to be sold. In the top right background, Guildford Cathedral on Stag Hill can just be made out. Today, the office building where the rearmost coaches stand, obscures the view. (*Safeguard Collection*)

Another Bedford VAM70/Willowbrook bus (UOR 603H) has a definite lean towards a Bristol LS in the Alder Valley fleet, while parked in Onslow Street bus station, in the early 1970s. Safeguard's office is in the background on the right. The Bristol LS had originated with Thames Valley, but had migrated southwards to Alder Valley's Southern Division. The latter's service 20 was a trunk route which previously would have normally been operated almost entirely with Dennis Loline double-deckers. (*MB Transport Photos*)

This is one of three new AEC Reliances with fifty-one-seat Willowbrook bodies purchased in 1971 to re-equip the Park Barn service. By the time of this view, the Farnham Road bus station stand arrangements had been altered and the site truncated by the new road bridge in the background over the River Wey. EPK 106J is accompanied by Alder Valley vehicles inherited from Thames Valley and Aldershot & District. (*The Bus Gallery*)

on Onslow Street itself, until the rebuilt bus station opened two months later. Subsequently, all of Safeguard's services were concentrated on the reduced Farnham Road site.

The first Safeguard vehicle to venture abroad was AEC Reliance coach GPA 112J in 1972, driven by John Lake, on a private hire charter to Switzerland for Weydon School in Farnham. Bert Newman was very much against the concept of his coaches going abroad and the trip had been sanctioned without his knowledge. However, despite whatever his reaction was, more Weydon School overseas work followed and it was the start of continental operations which have continued to this day. Various drivers tended to specialise in tours to specific countries – for example, John Lake and Andy Wilson to Switzerland and Stan Wickham to Holland.

Proposals were in place for a major re-organisation of hospital capacity in Guildford, with a new Guildford District Hospital to replace the Royal Surrey County Hospital in Farnham Road, as well as much of St Luke's Hospital. The new hospital was to be built on land between the A3 and the Westborough area, south of the railway line leading towards Ash. Prior to this, a new road known as Egerton Road, was built to serve as a hospital access, running from The Chase/Cathedral entrance roundabout across to Southway at its junction with Park Barn Drive. The new link road gave Safeguard the opportunity to introduce a supplementary 'express' or limited stop service on 24 December 1972 from the town centre to Park Barn, running non-stop until it reached Chapelhouse. Operated every thirty minutes on Mondays to Saturdays, it was given the designation 'Park Barn B', while the original service became 'Park Barn A'. The new 'B' service became very popular and was one-man operated from the outset. Prior to that, early in 1971, Safeguard's original Park Barn service had been extended further along Cabell Road to the shopping parade and back into Southway, effectively creating a circular arrangement through the estate. In common usage, the name Park Barn

had become more generally-accepted, thus this replaced Westborough on the destination blinds and on Safeguard's timetables.

The time-honoured name of the Aldershot & District Traction Co. Ltd disappeared from 1 January 1972, when it was changed to the Thames Valley & Aldershot Omnibus Co. Ltd, trading as Alder Valley. Under National Bus Co. auspices, Aldershot & District had been merged with the Thames Valley Traction Co. Ltd, based in Reading.

The 1973 brochure showed that Safeguard's long-established coastal express services were to Littlehampton and Bognor Regis (daily during the summer school holiday, except Mondays and Fridays) and to Worthing and Brighton (various levels of services between April and September, rising to daily during August). Both these started at Guildford and picked up at Shalford, Farncombe, Godalming, Milford, Witley, Chiddingfold and Northchapel. There was also the service acquired from Cooke's Coaches, on Saturdays from late May to mid-September to Ramsgate and Margate, from Stoughton, Guildford, Shalford, Chilworth, Shere and Gomshall. As well as many day and half-day excursions, holiday tours were offered to Scotland, the Lake District, the West Country, Wales and Blackpool for the Illuminations, after a battle to obtain licences. There were also three-day tours to Holland for the bulb fields and a four-day trip to the Rhine Valley in Germany. Again, specific drivers tended to concentrate on certain destinations, such as Nigel Cotton to North Wales or Steve Stonestreet to Scotland. This was appreciated by regular customers who brought much repeat business. The traditional Christmas Tour was also driven by Andy Wilson.

Since the late 1920s, Aldershot & District (and latterly Alder Valley) had also run summer coastal services from Brookwood, Woking, Guildford, Godalming and other points locally to places such as Brighton, Eastbourne, Hastings and Bognor Regis. From the 1974 season they were marketed under the National Express banner, being numbered 155 (Brighton and Hastings) and 156 (Bognor Regis). However, by the 1970s the popularity

Above left: Another 1971 AEC Reliance was FPC 15J, working on the limited-stop Park Barn 'B' service, which, as the notice in the window proclaims, was one-man operated. It is in Park Street which by then was totally altered from the appearance presented up to about 1970. This bus passed to Hutchings & Cornelius of South Petherton and then became yet another Safeguard vehicle to find its way to Safeway Services of the same village. (*M. King Collection*)

Above right: There were four heavyweight AEC Reliance coaches with J or K registration suffixes. GPA 112J was a forty-five-seat version of the Plaxton Panorama Elite and was the first Safeguard vehicle to undertake a trip abroad, on a Private Hire for Weydon School at Farnham. (*K. Wheal Collection*)

Right: AEC Reliance HPE 200K was fitted with jack-knife doors and a ticket machine, so it could qualify for New Bus Grant and be also used on one-man operated stage carriage services. It is emerging from the Farnham Road bus station onto Park Street, while operating the Park Barn 'B' service. (*PM Photography*)

Above left: Contemporary with HPE 200K was HPJ 999K, another AEC Reliance/Plaxton for coaching duties. Here it rests in the Southdown bus station at Bognor Regis, having arrived from the Guildford area on a summer coastal express service. (*N. Hamshere*)

Above right: Perhaps tempted by a coach dealer's salesman to try something different and economically priced, the Newman family took delivery in May 1972 of a Ford R1114 coach with a fifty-three-seat Duple Viceroy body. Not expected to stand up to long term use on touring work, it was more suited to day excursions, local contracts and coastal express duties and its blinds are set for the one to Brighton via Worthing. It was only kept until autumn 1973. (*T. W. Knowles*)

Left: Representing the six Bedford YRT/Duple Dominant fifty-three-seat coaches that arrived during 1973, is TPJ 780M. The photograph was taken in June 1974 at the Worthy Lane Coach Station in Winchester. Unlike earlier Bedfords, the 'Y' series featured an under-floor engine that allowed a better layout for the driver's area and the passenger entrance. (*M. Bennett*)

of such services was rapidly waning, with insufficient custom for two operators. Therefore, from the 1976 season these services were advertised as jointly operated by Safeguard and National Travel and licences were held by Safeguard and Alder Valley, while the Ramsgate/Margate service continued to be licensed just to Safeguard. They were extended to start from Woking; numbering was revised so that Bognor Regis became 154, Hastings 155 (and extended at times to Camber Sands) and Brighton & Eastbourne became 156. In due course, a feeder service into Woking from Ottershaw, Chertsey, Addlestone, Weybridge, Byfleet and Sheerwater was also jointly-licensed to Safeguard and Alder Valley. Also in 1976, a similar joint arrangement applied between National Travel and Whites Coaches of Camberley Ltd for summer services 157–160 from Camberley, Aldershot and Farnham to various coastal resorts stretching from Southsea to Hastings. The brochure for these carried Safeguard's name in addition, but they were not involved in their operation.

Some of the Dennisville journeys operated by Safeguard and some of those by Alder Valley on service 27 were extended by June 1973 along Egerton Road to the Ashenden Estate, thereby giving these services three outer termini. Beyond Dennisville, three Safeguard journeys then extended to the Cathedral, two at lunchtime to the University and nine to Ashenden Estate. From 24 February 1974, the Northway service was withdrawn on Sundays. On 29 September 1974, Alder Valley service 27 was renumbered 97 as part of a scheme to designate the services in Alder Valley's Aldershot Division, to avoid duplication with those of the erstwhile Thames Valley company.

The bus fleet was replaced in the early 1970s, starting in November 1969, with two Bedford VAM70/Willowbrook forty-five-seaters (UAA 751/2H), followed shortly afterwards by similar UOR 603H. The Transport Act 1968 contained provisions for a New Bus Grant scheme, whereby the government would pay up to 50 per cent of the cost of a bus or coach that would be used mainly on a stage carriage service and would achieve at least 50 per cent of its total mileage on such work in the first five years. The aforementioned Bedfords were the first vehicles that Safeguard received support for under this scheme. Advantage was taken of this subsidy when ordering new buses until the scheme was finally phased out in March 1984. However, these particular Bedford VAM70s were found to be unsuitable for the arduous requirements of the Westborough service, thus increasing maintenance costs.

1971 saw the replacement of the remaining earlier AEC Reliances with three of the same chassis with fifty-one-seat Willowbrook bodies – EPK 106/7J & FPC 15J. Coach fleet renewal continued with the arrival Bedford YRQ (forty-one/forty-five seats) and YRT (fifty-three-seat) models, although as a change, four heavyweight AEC Reliances also made an appearance. One of the latter forty-five-seaters – HPE 200K of 1972, was fitted with folding doors and a ticket machine, thus making this Plaxton Panorama Elite Express suitable for use on the bus services, qualifying it for New Bus Grant. Then, in April 1974 came a change in heavyweight chassis supplier with the arrival of VPF 42M, an attractive Willowbrook-bodied fifty-three-seat bus on a Leyland Leopard chassis. This vehicle introduced an ivory waistband to the bus livery, instead of cream. As the decade progressed, further Bedford and Leyland coaches were purchased, as well as eight Leopards with the Duple Dominant bus body over the years up to 1982.

Considerable extra daily work was found for some of the coaches in 1973 when the number of Surrey County Council school transport contracts successfully bid for saw an increase. Work for the Council's Education Department continued in varying amounts until recent years. In December 1975 Safeguard acquired a licence for certain excursions from Conway Hunt Ltd of Ottershaw, near Chertsey, thus extending their pick-up points into the Woking, Byfleet, Addlestone and Chertsey areas. The Conway Hunt

SAFEGUARD

1974
Golden Jubilee
Programme

BRIGHTON & WORTHING

Dates of operation:		
	April	Easter Sun. 14 and Easter Mon. 15.
	May	Sat. 25; Sun. 26; Mon. 27.
	June	Every Sunday.
	July	DAILY (Except Mondays or Fridays)
	August	EVERY DAY
	September	DAILY (Except Mondays or Fridays)

BOGNOR & LITTLEHAMPTON

Dates of operation: DAILY (Except Mondays or Fridays) from July 27 to 1 September

TIME TABLE FOR ABOVE SERVICES

GUILDFORD	*Library, North Street*	Dep. 0900	Arr. 2015
SHALFORD	*Station Bus Stop*	0910	
FARNCOMBE	*Opp. Kings Road*	0915	
GODALMING	*Coach Stop, Ockford Road*	0920	
MILFORD	*"Red Lion" P.H.*	0923	
WITLEY	*Star*	0925	
HAMBLEDON	*Lane End*	0929	
CHIDDINGFOLD	*Old Forge*	0935	
NORTH CHAPEL	*The Swan*	0945	
BOGNOR REGIS	*London Road Coach Park*	Arr. 1115	Dep. 1815
BRIGHTON		1115	1800
LITTLEHAMPTON	*Banjo Road*	1045	1845
WORTHING	*Steyne Gardens*	1045	1830

FARES

	From Guildford/Godalming (incl.)		Other Points	
	Adult	Child	Adult	Child
Single	50p	35p	50p	35p
Day Return	65p	45p	60p	40p
Period Return	90p	60p	85p	55p

Above left: From May 1974, the Leyland Leopard replaced the AEC Reliance as the Safeguard choice for heavyweight buses. Waiting in Farnham Road bus station to operate the Park Barn 'B' service is VPF 42M, with the last of the attractive Willowbrook bodies to be purchased. After seven to eight years of yeoman service around Guildford, this was another vehicle to migrate to Safeway Services of South Petherton. (*E. Kentell*)

Above right: From 1974, the Duple Dominant bus body became the Safeguard standard issue. The first one was GPA 853N in December of that year, a forty-five-seat model on a Bedford YRQ chassis, seen leaving Farnham Road bus station for Northway. (*R. C. Photos*)

Opposite left: 1974 marked Safeguard's Golden Jubilee, a milestone reflected in that year's tours, excursion and coastal express brochure. Bedford YRT OPK 132L is the coach, seen while on tour overseas.

Opposite right: This is the 1974 timetable and fares for the express services to the Sussex coastal resorts.

Above left: There were also several Leyland Leopard coaches, the first of which was HPG 29N with forty-nine-seat Duple Dominant body. Here it is outside the famous Cheltenham coach station while on hire to National Travel South West, probably as a duplicate on their service 790 Eastbourne–Cheltenham, which came through Guildford. (*Kevin Lane Collection*)

Above right: The first of several Leyland Leopard/Duple Dominant fifty-three-seat bus combinations was HPG 31N in spring 1975, about to set off on a Dennisville journey. (*Safeguard Collection*)

Left: The purchase of part of the business of Conway Hunt of Ottershaw in December 1975 included two Ford coaches, which Safeguard had no desire to keep and did not operate. This is FLB 482C, a Ford Thames 570E with forty-one-seat Duple Trooper body. Duple badged the 'Bella Vega' body as 'Trooper' when it was mounted on a Ford chassis. (*K. Wheal Collection*)

firm had been active for many years, formed in 1957 when Conway West Motors Ltd of Woking, established 1919, acquired W. S. Hunt's Coaches Ltd of Ottershaw, established by 1922. Two somewhat elderly Ford coaches were part of the deal, but being non-standard, were promptly disposed of by Safeguard. However, Conway Hunt continued running coaches for about another ten years, while the firm became Safeguard's booking agent in Ottershaw and at the Conway Hunt Travel Agency in Walton on Thames. An innovation in March 1976 was the acquisition by Safeguard of a twelve-seat Ford Transit minibus suitable for use on express, excursion and tour feeder services as well as for small private hire parties.

The new Guildford District Hospital finally opened on 16 October 1978. From the previous day, the joint Safeguard and Alder Valley service 97 had the journeys terminating at the entrance to Ashenden Estate

Above: Kit Newman with the first Ford Transit minibus acquired for small party private hire and for operating feeder trips for tours, excursions and coastal express services. KBL 110P was purchased in February 1976 after use by Reed of Maidenhead. It had a Williams Deansgate twelve-seat body conversion. (*Safeguard Collection*)

Left: One of two Leyland Leopard buses dating from spring 1976 was MPG 153P, seen arriving at a bus rally. Safeguard have attended a number of these rallies over the years, usually due to the willingness of certain drivers to visit such events on their day off. (*Safeguard Collection*)

Above left: During the 1970s and 1980s, Ken and Bern Newman would make the occasional second-hand coach purchase. HRN 684G was a forty-five-seat AEC Reliance/ Plaxton which spent the 1976 summer season with Safeguard. It was photographed in the livery of its original owner – Premier of Preston, Lancs. (*PM Photography*)

Above right: Artwork depicting a representation of some European destinations that were reached by Safeguard's coaches. (*Safeguard Collection*)

Below left: Leyland Leopard OPC 26R spent twelve years with Safeguard, including latterly a spell of use on service 550 from Aldershot to Camberley. On disposal it passed through a number of hands and is now preserved, as shown later in this book. (*Author's Collection*)

Below right: TPL 166S was the last Bedford 'lightweight' bus to be purchased – a fifty-three-seater on a YMT chassis, lasting until July 1987 when replaced by a Leyland Lynx. (*Author's Collection*)

Above left: The last Safeguard Bedford YMT/Duple Dominant combination (later YMT and YNT Bedfords had Plaxton bodywork) was TPL 167S from September 1977. In this view it was parked at The Duke's Mound end of Brighton's Madeira Drive on the seafront on 11 May 1978. (*Safeguard Collection*)

Above right: This is UPH 109S, a 1977 Leyland Leopard with forty-nine-seat Plaxton Supreme bodywork, working an extended or holiday tour, at Aust Services on the M4. The Supreme body had replaced the Panorama Elite. (*K. Wheal Collection*)

Right: Replacing KBL 110P as the 'baby' of the fleet was XPH 539T, another Ford Transit but with Tricentrol body conversion. In this view, it has probably acted as a 'feeder' for an excursion and is in North Street, Guildford, by the library. (*N. Hamshere*)

extended along Egerton Road to a point near the hospital. These journeys no longer double-ran to serve St Johns Road and as the remaining hourly Sunday journeys worked by Alder Valley went to the hospital, St. Johns Road and the Cathedral forecourt were not served on that day. By August 1979, the off-peak frequency on Mondays to Saturdays on Park Barn A service was reduced from every twelve to every twenty minutes. The Park Barn B service stopped additionally at Guildford Park Road, for the railway station and at the District Hospital.

Above: Photographed outside of the garage at Ridgemount was VDV 97S, a Bedford VAS5 with Duple Dominant twenty-nine-seat body, purchased in December 1978 from Seward's Coaches of Dalwood, deep in rural east Devon. (*Safeguard Collection*)

Right: This map from the London Country timetable booklet of January 1978 reflects Safeguard's second service to Park Barn via Guildford Park and Egerton Road and also the extension of some of Safeguard's and Alder Valley's Dennisville journeys to the University of Surrey or the entrance to the Ashenden estate.

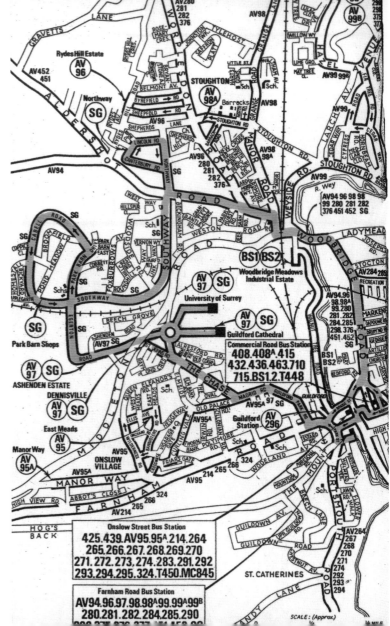

SERVICE CO-ORDINATION AND COACHING FREEDOM

Major re-development in Guildford town centre saw the building of the Friary Shopping Centre, on what had been the old Friary Brewery site, together with an adjacent bus station to accommodate all services. The latter comprised a mixture of herringbone-style drive-in, reverse-out stands alongside the shopping centre and some conventional stops on the adjacent Commercial Road. At last, from 2 November 1980, Guildford had a bus station that could accommodate all services in one location, allowing the closure of the Onslow Street, Farnham Road and original Commercial Road sites. To replace Safeguard's office at the Onslow Street site, a new building was constructed on part of the yard at Ridgemount, with a store, office and other facilities on the ground floor and more offices and a Boardroom upstairs. A new 10,000 gallon underground fuel tank and a steel roller-shutter garage door were installed. Although the company's registered office was transferred to Ridgemount, Safeguard rented a booking and enquiry office in the new Friary Bus Station to maintain a presence in the town centre, which also acted as a bus driver rest facility.

The late 1970s saw the initiation of a nationwide project by the National Bus Co. subsidiaries, in conjunction with local subsidising authorities.

This was known as the Market Analysis Project (MAP), designed to measure patronage to determine which services or journeys were well-used and those that were not, by extensive collection of survey data. This applied to both urban and rural areas, although services to the latter were more vulnerable as subsidy costs were often higher. The aim of MAP was to reduce the call for revenue support from the public purse, resulting in network reductions, fewer vehicles and drivers and sometimes garage closures. Networks were segmented by what could be run from one depot and given local identities, which were often regarded as somewhat twee or contrived. Most local services operated by Alder Valley and London Country were branded 'Weyfarer', a logo for which was applied to the vehicles and publicity material. Although this chiefly affected the NBC companies, the local Guildford independent operators were also involved. After much planning and negotiation, Alder Valley's Guildford town services were renumbered, restructured and some much-reduced from 31 August 1980, with some re-distribution of responsibility. Also introduced at this time was a Guildford Travelwide ticket that offered unlimited travel for various periods on all bus services within the defined town area.

Displaying the refreshed coach livery of red, ivory and grey is Bedford YMT/Plaxton Supreme coach YPB 837T, new in January 1979. (*K. Wheal Collection*)

DPD 33T arrived four months later, with a Duple Dominant body on a Bedford YLQ chassis. This was the penultimate forty-five-seat coach to be acquired. Vehicles of that capacity were tending to be less favoured from that time onwards and were phased out of production, as a fifty-three-seat vehicle gave additional flexibility and money-earning potential, for a negligible difference in fuel consumption. (*K. Wheal Collection*)

Originally, Alder Valley intended to withdraw from the Guildford Park area, against which Safeguard withdrew their Northway service after 30 August, it being incorporated into the Alder Valley service to Rydes Hill Estate, which was numbered 231. However, Alder Valley changed its plans and the joint service to Dennisville and the District Hospital continued, but was reduced to an hourly frequency by each company on Mondays to Saturdays with the bifurcations to the Cathedral and University withdrawn. It was extended from the town centre to Stoke Road and Bellfields Estate, to terminate at Hazel Avenue. Alder Valley used the number 229, while there was also an hourly Alder Valley 230 from Onslow Village to Bellfields via the town centre, to maintain the twenty minute interval service to Bellfields. The Safeguard journeys were diverted in Dennisville to serve St John's Road, but only on the way to the Hospital, presumably to assist those returning from town with shopping. The Park Barn services were largely unaffected, although the 'B' gained an extra stop at Elmside in Dennisville. The fact that Alder Valley received subsidy for their services to Bellfields, whereas Safeguard did not, was a matter of extreme irritation for the latter.

For some while, the only remaining crew-operated buses in Guildford were on the Park Barn A service at certain times. This came to an end in March 1981 with the retirement of Betty Ball, Peggy Dobbs and Doris Jefferies, the last Safeguard conductresses. The evening peak frequency on this service was reduced to every twenty minutes, leaving just the morning peak at every twelve minutes. By 13 November 1982, one journey per hour on Park Barn A on Sunday afternoons was diverted at Southway/Egerton Road to double-run to the District Hospital (shortly to be formally named Royal Surrey County Hospital) while by 30 June 1984, the whole Sunday service was halved in frequency to every forty minutes.

Betty Ball had worked for Aldershot & District for a few months before joining Safeguard. Bill Clifton asked her mother-in-law whether Betty would like a job, which she took as the garage was more convenient to where she lived. She enjoyed being a conductress and recalls some of the 'characters' among the regular passengers, such as the football fans who would be picked up in Woodbridge Road after matches and the man who would play the spoons on the bus after an evening spent in the Woodbridge Hill Club. When the A3 road ran by the Wooden Bridge (along Ladymead and Midleton Road), there would be great traffic jams at summer weekends at this bottle-neck and it could take thirty minutes to get to Westborough. At quiet times she would do knitting on the bus and managed to produce a set of woolly hats for an entire football team. Whatever happened, she carried on working; on one occasion she became sick with a migraine, got off her bus and went home, but recovered enough to get back on it when it returned from Westborough on the next trip, so she could complete her shift.

Meanwhile, there were some important legislative changes affecting service licensing. The Transport Act 1980, promoted by the recently-elected Conservative government, included in its provisions the abolition of the need for a Road Service Licence in respect of excursions, tours and longer-distance express services. This deregulatory move meant that it was far easier for operators like Safeguard to introduce new day trips or extended tours to capitalise on commercial opportunities, or to amend or cancel them as demand required, as well as the avoidance of mountains of paperwork and the tedious business of fighting one's case in front of objectors in the Traffic Court. For stage carriage activities, applications for new or amended services, or to cancel them, were normally granted automatically, as a potential objector had to prove that the proposals were against the public interest, rather than the applicant having to prove that they were in the public interest, as had been the case since 1931.

For the 1980 season, the summer express coastal services were the 154 to Littlehampton and Bognor Regis (August only), the 155 to Seaford,

Eastbourne, Bexhill and Hastings via Cranleigh, Horsham and Lewes (Saturdays), the 156 to Worthing and Brighton, extended to Eastbourne on Wednesdays and Sundays and the 159 to Ramsgate and Margate via Dorking and Canterbury (Saturdays). For 1981, the 159 had gained a feeder service from Camberley, Aldershot and Farnham, the 154 had been replaced by periodic excursions and there was a new 153 from Leatherhead, Bookham and Guildford to Southampton and Bournemouth on Saturdays, described in the brochure as a joint service in conjunction with Epsom Coaches (H. R. Richmond Ltd) and operated by the latter. By comparison, in 1984 the 153 had disappeared, replaced by a 157 from Woking, Guildford, Aldershot & Farnham to Christchurch, Boscombe and Bournemouth on Saturdays. The 155 and 156 were actually licensed as stage carriage services from 1982.

In 1984, Safeguard celebrated its Diamond Jubilee, with the publication by the company of a short illustrated booklet written by John Sutton and Norman Hamshere. Incidentally, John hand-built his own collection of model Safeguard vehicles, later housed at Guildford Museum. Appropriately, two new vehicles in 1984 had '60' in their registration mark – Bedford YNT/Plaxton A60 FPD and Mercedes Benz L608D nineteen-seater A60 GPL. In its sixtieth year, Safeguard had nineteen vehicles, with a peak vehicle requirement on the bus services of six, of which five were used all day. 200,000 bus miles per year were run, carrying over one million passengers and bringing in £307,000 in revenue. No subsidy was required from the County Council. There were nine bus drivers, ten coach drivers and eight other staff. The busiest bus service in town was Safeguard's Park Barn A, doubtless reflecting the relatively low average household income, 42 per cent of households with no car and the relatively low fares charged. A single from Park Barn to town was 34p, whereas by comparison, Bellfields to town was 50p for a comparable distance. Park Barn was home to 5,700 people.

Unfortunately, shortly afterwards, in January 1985, there occurred the death at the age of eighty-two of the last of the founding brothers – Albert Newman, having retired from active daily involvement in the business in the early 1970s. He was survived by his wife, Ethel, who lived to the age of 102 and passed away in 2001. Ethel's maiden name was Sharp and her father, also Albert, was a coal merchant and her brothers were haulage contractors. Albert Sharp became the landlord of the Rowbarge public house near the Stoughton Road in 1922 and by that time he was also operating a Garford charabanc, thus pre-empting the Newmans' similar activities by a few years.

Looking back now, it is recalled that Bert, known to his family as Pop, was a popular person whose real pleasure was driving a coach, but he never did so again after an accident that was not his fault. He was a keen vegetable gardener, kept chickens and rabbits and liked deep-sea angling. He also liked a beer or two and was well known in many of Guildford's hostelries and, some say, seemingly in most of the pubs across southern England, which were refreshment stops on coach excursions. Such stops were popular with both passengers and drivers and very often there would be free beer and cigarettes dispensed to the driver by the landlord, paid for by Bert Newman. It is said that coach trip itineraries were navigated by pub name. Brian Williams recalls that at Brighton one day, Bert suddenly appeared unannounced and treated all the Safeguard drivers to a free dinner with drinks in a pub, where he was obviously known. There were no concerns about imbibing in those days! Quite often Bert was at the garage with quantities of cigarettes or sweets to be given to employees and it is said that 'Bert's Boys' were always looked after. However narrow the entrance to the garage was, thereby making it difficult to get the vehicles in, many remember Bert's often-repeated phrase: 'I can get them through'.

After Bert's death, Safeguard was controlled by his two sons, Bern and Ken, while Bern's son, Graham, became a shareholder in June 1985, having

Above left: Leyland Leopard FPA 584V is about to leave a hotel on a holiday tour, presumably in 1984 when Safeguard celebrated its Diamond Jubilee. (*G. Button Collection*)

Above right: Pembroke Broadway by Camberley station is the location of Leyland Leopard bus GPG 342V, laying over between trips on Surrey County Council contracted service 550 to Aldershot, which Safeguard ran from October 1986 until August 1992. (*K. Wheal Collection*)

Right: Acquired in 1980 from Glenton Tours of London was AJD 164T, a Leyland Leopard with forty-five-seat Plaxton Supreme bodywork. Glenton operated upmarket extended tours which were popular with American clientele and for some years specified that Plaxton supply them with coaches with a centre entrance to special order, although this coach was more conventional. (*K. Wheal Collection*)

Above left: Safeguard's sixth Leyland Leopard/Duple Dominant bus was NPD 689W, new in February 1981, seen here heading into Guildford down Farnham Road in June 1988. (*R. Kirwin*)

Above right: On the day of their retirement in March 1981, left to right we see long-serving conductresses Betty Ball, Peggy Dobbs and Doris Jeffries, the last 'clippies' in Guildford. (*B. Ball Collection*)

Left: TPA 968X was yet another Leyland Leopard bus, seen in Camberley on service 550. New in December 1981, it was operated until 1992. Visible in the bus is an Almex ticket machine – a system that had replaced the Setright machines on Safeguard services. (*Author*)

started work in the business back in February 1973, preferring workshop activities to office tasks. After leaving school, the careers of Graham and his cousin David had followed quite different paths. Graham decided to join the family business after completing an engineering apprenticeship at Grays Trucks in Guildford. However, David went to college to study antique furniture restoration and became skilled at working with wood. Although he was to hold shares, he did not seek an active role in Safeguard, not attending Board meetings until more recently, feeling that it is sometimes hard to have simultaneous good paternal and business relationships. Ken Newman supported his son's decision. Gordon Button replaced Bill Clifton as Company Secretary, on the latter's retirement from 2 August 1985, just short of fifty years' service to the company in various capacities.

Vehicle-wise, the first half of the 1980s saw the delivery of Leyland Leopard buses and Bedford YMT/YNT coaches. Also purchased were examples of the Leyland Tiger, the first being a Plaxton-bodied coach (UPG 349X) in May 1982. This was the first vehicle of 12m length in the fleet, which introduced a revised livery in which ivory predominated over red. A powerful Leyland Tiger/Duple Dominant bus (C164 SPB) arrived in November 1985, which in order to gain a discount, had been ordered in conjunction with a similar bus (C195 WJT) for Tillingbourne Bus Co. of Cranleigh. Interestingly, the AEC Reliance returned to the fleet in September 1985 when UGB 14R, with a Duple Dominant bus body, was acquired from Tillingbourne, having been new to Hutchison of Overtown in Scotland. It was also unusual for a second-hand bus to be purchased.

This is perhaps an appropriate point to recount a few miscellaneous anecdotes of Safeguard coaching work in the 1970s and 1980s. Attitudes of officialdom to certain practices were more relaxed then.

- On long trips requiring two drivers, it was common practice to change drivers on the move, at speeds of up to 65 mph on the Motorway. One would slide into the seat and take over the pedals and steering wheel, while the other got out the other side. The passengers took this in their stride, although it was more challenging with one of the Bedfords with the engine cover alongside the driver's seat. During a rest period, the second driver would sleep on the back seat, which was partitioned off with a makeshift curtain on a rail for privacy;
- Many coach companies would run Excursions for the Illuminations at Blackpool – up and back in a single day. All would leave the resort around 6 p.m., resulting in a convoy of up to 200 coaches heading onto the Motorway. The police took little interest – they were just keen to get the often inebriated day trippers out of the town before they caused trouble;
- On a trip to an England-Scotland football match in Glasgow, there were barrels in the boot of the coach, with the beer piped to a makeshift bar on the rear seat. Eight barrels had been consumed before arrival in Glasgow. The coach door was opened for a police check and spilt beer trickled down the coach steps in front of the officer who turned round and walked away!
- Driver Geoff Attwell always took a bottle of Bristol Cream sherry with him on tour, after disappointment on his first trip when the hotel did not have any;
- During the Miners' Strike in 1984, Safeguard was taking Guildford-based officers of Surrey Constabulary to and from the Nottingham area, with the coaches and drivers staying there all week to ferry them around. The convoy of coaches returning to Surrey on the Friday evening would travel at a constant 80 mph in the fast lane of the M1, with a only few feet of road space between them. Everyone wanted to get home as quickly as possible. There were no tachographs or speed limiters then and the sight of a coach full of uniforms meant

Above left: The first example of a Leyland Tiger in the fleet was UPG 349X with fifty-three-seat Plaxton Supreme bodywork. In 1982 it was also the first 12m vehicle and the first in a modernised livery featuring stripes, with no grey and where ivory predominates over red. (*PM Photography*)

Above right: YPD 217Y was the last new Leyland Leopard bus in November 1982. Together with NPD 689W, it left the fleet in September 1992, after the loss of the contract to provide Camberley-Aldershot service 550. (*K. Wheal Collection*)

Below left: Two Bedford YNTs with the recently-introduced Plaxton Paramount bodies were delivered in spring 1983. This one, in Guildford's Friary Bus Station was actually BPC 227Y, but was photographed carrying temporarily the incorrect registration of BPC 277Y, which was an error. (*Safeguard Collection*)

Below right: Another Bedford YNT/Plaxton Paramount was A60 FPD, delivered in Safeguard's Diamond Jubilee year, appropriately carrying a registration number commensurate with the occasion. It is parked in Plymouth's Bretonside bus station and displays another coach livery alteration featuring slanting stripes. (*J. Law*)

Above: This Mercedes Benz L608D had nineteen-seat bodywork by Reeve Burgess. A60 GPL also dated from 1984 and was used primarily for small private hire parties. (*Author*)

Right: Posing for his photograph in front of Leyland Tiger A62 HPG is driver Ted Yarham. (*Safeguard Collection*)

that the motorway traffic patrols suffered temporary blindness and amnesia;

- Safeguard were contracted by Coldingley Prison at Bisley to take inmates with warders to the Law Courts in London, usually in a minibus. The prisoners were handcuffed to the seats, but one day, one of them managed to get out of the restraints as driver Bill Bishop was nearing Lambeth Bridge. The prisoner knocked out the warder and moved to the front of the minibus in order to jump out the door. However, Bill said 'I'm not having an escape on my bus' and promptly terminated the attempt by immobilising the prisoner with a fire extinguisher.

Above: This Leyland Tiger had Duple's Caribbean bodywork, which was a one-off in the Safeguard fleet. This coach memorably let in rain water through its roof during a Scottish tour and had to be repaired while away, by a local Duple dealer. Displaying yet another striped livery variation, it stands alongside an Alder Valley Bristol VR double-decker, just arrived in Guildford on service 271 from Chiddingfold. (*PM Photography*)

Left: Acquired in June 1985, Leyland Tiger/Plaxton Paramount coach UTN 956Y had been new to Moordale Coaches of Newcastle Upon Tyne. (*Safeguard Collection*)

THE GUILDFORD BUS STUDY AND DEREGULATION

The finances of Alder Valley and London Country were not in good shape, with high overhead costs; many of their Surrey bus services, both urban and rural, were in receipt of substantial amounts of revenue support from Surrey County Council. Tillingbourne Bus Co. had for some time a desire to seek support from the Council for the transfer of loss-making Alder Valley and London Country services radiating south and south-east from Guildford, to itself. It claimed it could run them without subsidy as operating costs were lower. The Council was interested but suggested that a wider approach might be necessary. Therefore, Tillingbourne encouraged Safeguard and Blue Saloon to come to the table, where a plan was formulated for Safeguard and Blue Saloon to take over the Guildford town services, while Tillingbourne would acquire certain rural and inter-urban services. By such route transfer, either the Alder Valley or London Country garage in Guildford could be closed and the remaining operations combined on one site, leading to substantial fixed cost savings.

Alder Valley and London Country naturally counter-responded, claiming the 'consortium' of independents' proposals were unrealistic. They put forward their own proposals whereby they would take over Safeguard's services and most of Tillingbourne's, even though Safeguard received no revenue support. In order to inform its Highways & Transport Committee, the County Council engaged a consultant to produce an impartial report. When their work was 80 per cent complete, the government published a White Paper which outlined its intention to radically change the way bus services were provided, through deregulation and privatisation. Thus, any route transfer carefully engineered by the Council, might have been undermined in two years time by legislation allowing open competition.

Notwithstanding such concerns, when the report was published, it came out in favour of the independents' proposals and was adopted by the Council. However, the Council was not in a position to order route transfer from one operator to another – it would have to be achieved by negotiation between the companies and in order to encourage this, the Council proposed to suspend all revenue support payments. There then followed much discussion and negotiation between all of the parties – ranging from the amicable to the somewhat hostile.

Above left: Bert (aka Pop), the last of the founding Newman brothers, passed away in January 1985, aged eighty-two. Loved by his family and respected by his loyal long-serving drivers as a benevolent employer and friend, here is Bert on holiday in Devon indulging in one of his noted interests. (*Newman Family Collection*)

Above right: Bill Clifton retired in August 1985 after just short of fifty years service with Safeguard in various roles, latterly as Company Secretary – a remarkable employment record. He was photographed with Ruby Franklin who also worked for Safeguard, as a book-keeper. (*Safeguard Collection*)

Left: Advantageously ordered at the same time as a similar bus by Tillingbourne Bus Co., C164 SPB was Safeguard's only Leyland Tiger bus to be bought new (in November 1985); it had a similar Duple Dominant body to those on the Leyland Leopards. It is picking up passengers at Woking, displaced from trains due to engineering work. Happily it still exists, after use in Scotland, being owned since 2007 by Richard Kirwin. (*Author's Collection*)

Service 559 – Byfleet – Sheerwater

Byfleet, Clock House	0749	0810	Sheerwater, Lambourne Cr.	1545
Manor Farm, Sanway Rd	0753	0813	Maybury Hill, College Rd	1550
West Byfleet, corner	0801	0821	Maybury, Maybury Inn	1552
Pyrford, Village Hall	..	0826	Pyrford, Village Hall	1558
Maybury, Maybury Inn	..	0832	West Byfleet, corner	1603
Maybury Hill, College Rd	..	0834	Manor Farm, Sanway Rd	1611
Sheerwater, Lambourne Cr	..	0840	Byfleet, Clockhouse	1615

Service 550 – Aldershot – Tongham – Ash – Ash Vale – Frimley – Camberley

Mondays – Saturdays

	N s											
All Hallows Sch									1508*			
Aldershot, The Grove	..	0800	0900	1000	1100	1200	1300	1400	1515	1620	1703	1800
Ash Rd, P/Wales	..	0807	0907	1007	1107	1207	1307	1407	1552	1627	1710	1807
Tongham, Manor Rd	..	0810	0910	1010	1110	1210	1310	1410	1525	1630	1713	1810
Tongham, Poyle Rd	0710		0913	1013	1113	1213	1313	1413			1716	1813
Ash Green, Old Stn	0715		0918	1018	1118	1218	1318	1418			1721	1818
Ash, Station	0718		0921	1021	1121	1221	1321	1421			1724	1821
Ash, Greyhound		0813							1528	1633		
Ash, Wharfinger	0722	0817	0925	1025	1125	1225	1325	1425	1532	1637	1728	1825
Ash Vale, Stn	0726	0821	0929	1029	1129	1229	1329	1429	1536	1641	1732	1829
Mytchett Cross Rds	0729	0824	0932	1032	1132	1232	1332	1432	1539	1644	1735	1832
Frimley Grn, Rose & Th	0733	0828	0936	1036	1136	1236	1336	1436	1543	1648	1739	1836
Frimley, Church Rd	0740	0835	0943	1043	1143	1243	1343	1443	1550	1655	1746	1843
Frimley Park Hospital	0741	P	0944	1044	1144	1244	1344	1444	1551	1656	1747	..
Warren Est, Longmeadow	0744		0947	1047	1147	1247	1347	1447	1554	1659	1750	..
Ravenswood R/about	0746		0949	1049	1149	1249	1349	1449	1556	1701	1752	..
Camberley, Rail Stn	0750	0843	0953	1053	1153	1253	1353	1453	1600	1705	1756	..

	N s											
Camberley, Rail Stn	..	0755	0900	1000	1100	1200	1300	1400	1535	1605	1710	1758
Ravenswood Roundabout	..	0759	0904	1004	1104	1204	1304	1404	P	P	1714	1802
Warren Est, Longmeadow	..	0801	0906	1006	1106	1206	1306	1406	P	P	1716	1804
Frimley Park Hospital	..	0804	0909	1009	1109	1209	1309	1409			1719	1807
Frimley, Church Rd	0715	0805	0910	1010	1110	1210	1310	1410	1543	1613	1720	1808
Frimley Grn, Rose & Th	0720	0810	0915	1015	1115	1215	1315	1415	1548	1618	1725	1813
Mytchett, Cross Rds	0724	0814	0919	1019	1119	1219	1319	1419	1552	1622	1729	1817
Ash Vale, Stn	0727	0817	0922	1022	1122	1222	1322	1422	1555	1625	1732	1820
Ash, Wharfinger	0731	0821	0926	1026	1126	1226	1326	1426	1559	1629	1736	1824
Ash, Greyhound		0825							1603			
Ash Station	0735		0930	1030	1130	1230	1330	1430		1633	1740	1828
Ash Green, Old Stn	0737		0933	1033	1133	1233	1333	1433		1636	1743	1831
Tongham, Poyle Rd	0742		0938	1038	1138	1238	1338	1438		1641	1748	1836
Tongham, Manor Rd	0745	0828	0941	1041	1141	1241	1341	1441	1606	1644	1751	..
Ash Rd, P/Wales	0748	0831	0944	1044	1144	1244	1344	1444	1609	1647	1754	..
Aldershot, The Grove	0755	0838	0951	1051	1151	1251	1351	1451	1616	1654	1800	..
All Hallows Sch		0845*										

N s....NOT Saturdays   *....Schooldays ONLY   P....operates via Park Road, Camberley

Above: Leyland Tiger/Plaxton Paramount C270 TPL was acquired in March 1986 and later carried the registration DSK 560. It was the first Safeguard coach to be fitted with a toilet and double glazing, allowing it to be termed as an 'executive' coach, a considerable advance in marketing terms. Note the Christmas decorations for 1987 on the dashboard – the work of driver Nigel Cotton. (*R. Kirwin*)

Right: Timetables for Surrey County Council contracted services 550 and 559, at the implementation of 'Deregulation' in October 1986.

Safeguard's second Leyland Tiger bus was KUS 244Y, previously owned by Hutchisons of Overtown in Scotland. Seen here in Guildford's Friary Bus Station, it is showing service G3 to Bellfields Estate as a destination. Sold in November 2001, it and C164 SPB were the last high-floor buses in the fleet. (*Safeguard Collection*)

In November 1986, the Volvo B10M chassis made its first appearance in the Safeguard coach fleet. B907 SPR, seen in April 1990, was one of a pair with fifty-three-seat Plaxton Paramount bodywork to be purchased from the well-known coaching firm of Excelsior from Bournemouth, remaining for just under ten years. (*R. Kirwin*)

The details of the final outcome in terms of service changes are largely outside the scope of this story, but London Country kept their Guildford town services and Alder Valley most of theirs. Safeguard had proposed in 1984 to retain Park Barn service B every twenty minutes, with an hourly extension on a circular route, clockwise and anti-clockwise to Fairlands, Wood Street and Rydes Hill, in order to replace subsidised Alder Valley services. This would have been run without subsidy during the day on Mondays to Saturdays, if Surrey County Council was willing to give a long term guarantee for Safeguard's school contract work. However, what actually happened from 14 April 1985 was that Park Barn A was numbered G4, with the morning peak frequency reduced to every twenty minutes as applied for the rest of the day, while Park Barn B was unaltered, being renumbered G5. The latter now served all stops en-route as the old 229 service through Guildford Park and Dennisville to the hospital was withdrawn. The town centre to Bellfields part of erstwhile services 229/230 became a separate service G3 running every twenty minutes Mondays to Saturdays. Operated jointly by Safeguard and Alder Valley, each company operated every forty minutes. In addition, Safeguard worked the morning journey on new school service G12, previously part of Alder Valley 244, from Fairlands and Wood Street Green to Park Barn School, which had been part of their original proposal.

Commencing on 1 October 1985 for the new Sainsbury store at Burpham, was a service for shoppers on Mondays to Saturdays. Operated by London Country, Alder Valley and Safeguard in rotation in successive weeks, it started at Park Barn and served Rydes Hill Estate, Stoughton and Bellfields, all areas not directly linked to Burpham by ordinary bus services. Not very successful, it was withdrawn after Christmas Eve the same year. From 10 February 1986, both G4 and G5 were diverted once per hour during the off-peak period on Mondays to Fridays via Park Barn Drive and Barnwood Road, before resuming their usual route in Cabell Road. This gave the upper end of the Park Barn Estate a service for the first time.

John Amphlett passed away in May 1986, marking the end of a link with Safeguard's incorporation. At that time he was still officially Company Chairman but had not attended meetings for a few years previously; he still held one share which remains in his name to this day.

The previously mentioned White Paper published in 1984 ultimately led to the introduction of the Transport Act 1985. One of its key provisions, along with the sale of National Bus Co. subsidiaries to the private sector by a bidding process, was that bus services would no longer require a Road Service Licence. Under normal circumstances, no objections could be lodged and Hearings would no longer be held. Instead, operators had to register their intention to start, change or cancel a service at least forty-two days in advance of the planned implementation date. They could therefore control the commercial destiny of services which were to be run without local authority financial support. The term 'stage carriage service' was replaced with 'local bus service'. In spring 1986, operators had to register the level of service they wished to run on a commercial basis from 26 October 1986, the date when the Act became effective. The local authorities could then decide whether they wished to supplement them by securing 'socially-necessary' services, mainly through a competitive tendering process.

Safeguard registered services G3 (perpetuating the joint operation with Alder Valley), G4 and G5 for operation from 26 October – which came to be known as D-Day. On Sundays, buses on the G4 to Park Barn via Woodbridge Road returned to Guildford as G5 via the hospital and Guildford Park and vice versa. An hourly frequency was provided on both of the resulting circuits, clockwise and anti-clockwise. During the summer of 1986, Safeguard put in bids to Surrey County Council to operate under contract some services not registered by Alder Valley or London Country.

The contract to provide the bus to Park Barn School from Fairlands and Wood Street passed to Newtons Coaches from D-Day and was re-numbered 535. However, Safeguard were successful in being awarded contracts to run three additional services in places somewhat removed from their traditional stamping ground of the Guildford urban area. The first of these was the 546, with a Monday to Saturday peak hour trip from Elstead, Shackleford, Hurtmore and Charterhouse to Godalming in the morning and back in the evening. There was also a round trip in the morning for shoppers from Shackleford to Godalming on Tuesdays, Wednesdays, Fridays and Saturdays. These were replacements for Alder Valley 246, as that service had been reduced to a Monday and Thursday shoppers bus from Elstead to Godalming. However, Alder Valley still ran some journeys commercially between Elstead and Godalming (272) while Blue Saloon competed with them with a service numbered 6, but both of these ran via Milford rather than Shackleford. In due course, Safeguard normally used a twenty-seat Mercedes minibus (D159 HML) on the 546.

The most substantial contract gained, after Safeguard offered the lowest-priced tender of the four bids made, was for a service 550, to replace Alder Valley service 450. It will be noted that Surrey County Council gave 5xx numbers to their contracted services. The 550 ran hourly, Mondays to Saturdays, from Aldershot to Camberley via Tongham, Ash Green, Ash, Ash Wharf, Ash Vale, Mytchett, Frimley Green, Frimley, Frimley Park Hospital and Ravenswood. Certain journeys operated between Tongham and Ash Wharf via Manor Road and Shawfield Road and between Frimley and Camberley via Park Road, principally to cater for schools traffic, while on schooldays there was also an extension from Aldershot to All Hallows School in Weybourne. Also secured was service 559 on schooldays from Byfleet, West Byfleet and Pyrford to Bishop David Brown School at Sheerwater, previously operated by London Country as 837. The regular drivers on this school service were Malcolm Toghill and Alan Belcher.

The coastal express services continued to be reduced, in line with declining patronage. For 1986, the offer was: 154 to Bognor Regis and Littlehampton (on two Thursdays in August), 155 to Brighton, Seaford and Eastbourne (Wednesdays 16 July – 27 August, Saturdays 24 May – 4 October, when it was extended to Hastings), 156 to Worthing and Brighton (second Tuesday between May and October, every Tuesday 29 July – 26 August and Thursdays 31 July – 28 August) and 157 Bournemouth (Saturdays 28 June – 13 September). This further reduced for 1987 to: 155 to Worthing and Brighton (second Tuesday between May and October, every Tuesday and Thursday during the summer school holiday and Saturdays 30 May – 3 October, when it was extended to Eastbourne): 156 Brighton and Eastbourne (Wednesdays 15 July – 2 September): 157 to Bournemouth (Saturdays 27 June – 19 September).

Using the freedoms of the Transport Act 1985, a supplementary commercial town service was started in May 1987, initially numbered G10, which also included odd journeys via Normandy to Ash, to facilitate driver changes on service 550. This service went through a multitude of permutations, with changes sometimes coming every few months, using variously the numbers G9, 10, 11 and 12. Usually operated by a Mercedes Benz 609D twenty-seat bus or a twenty-five-seat Optare City Pacer on a Volkswagen chassis, these services were designed to serve some of the narrower residential roads, complementing the G4/G5 main services. Areas covered for varying periods between 1987 and 1994 by these convoluted and complex routes included Westway and Foxburrows Avenue in Westborough, Northway, Grange Park, Rydes Hill Estate and Broadacres, as well as Applegarth Avenue, Pond Meadows and Clover Road in Park Barn. A service G9 covering Northway and Grange Park was introduced in August 1987 to replace withdrawn Alder Valley services 9 and 15. However, ultimately, they failed to capture sufficient patronage or enough support to sustain them commercially, although they may have

Above left: Mercedes Benz 609D bus D159 HML, with twenty-seat Reeve Burgess bodywork, was purchased in April 1987 for use on rural service 546 in the Godalming area and for the new Guildford local services around various small residential roads. Here it is on Northway service G10, sometime between 1988 and 1991. (*K. Wheal Collection*)

Above right: The newly-available Leyland Lynx offered a reduction in step height and better accessibility than the earlier Leopards and Tigers. D165 HML was, in June 1987, the first of four in the fleet. The forty-nine-seat body was also by Leyland. In March 1988 it runs along Egerton Road in Guildford, past the future site of the Tesco store. (*R. Kirwin*)

Right: E297 OMG was one of a pair of Leyland Lynx dating from May 1988, which were usurped in September 1998 by a pair of smaller, pre-owned, Dennis Darts. All four of Safeguard's Lynx buses subsequently passed to Damory Coaches in Dorset. (*R. Kirwin*)

served as a barrier to some, but by no means all, competitive intrusion into an area of town that Safeguard still regarded as its own. To describe all the changes to G9-12 would be tedious, so they are listed in Appendix 1, along with more detail of all Safeguard's services from 1986 to the present.

A competitive intervention was launched into Safeguard's core territory on 23 February 1987, when Blue Saloon adjusted their service G2 which ran from the town centre to Grange Park. It was made into a circular route, also covering Guildford Park, the hospital, Park Barn Drive and Rydes Hill, to which was added the Northway area on 3 August, the same day as Safeguard's new service G9 started.

From 12 May 1987 the four days per week shoppers' journeys on service 546 were extended from Godalming to Guildford but the contract for the whole service ceased in October that year. At the end of January 1988, economies were made on Sundays on the Park Barn services, by withdrawing G5 via Guildford Park on that day and by diverting again some G4 journeys via Royal Surrey County Hospital.

In the new 'Deregulated' environment, there was thought by some that in urban areas, high frequency services operated with sixteen or twenty-seat minibuses, were the way forward. Operating costs were considered to be lower, including in some cases drivers' wages; with closely-spaced journeys it was hoped that the public would just be able to 'turn up and go', without remembering a timetable. In 1988, Safeguard carefully considered the cost and logistical implications of this when Alder Valley proposed that the two companies convert their operations to the Bellfields Estate to a minibus service running every ten minutes on weekdays, with an extension to Guildford Station, however, this was ultimately not pursued.

The summer of 1988 was the last in which the timetabled coastal services ran: 155 to Brighton and Eastbourne on Saturdays and on Wednesdays in the school holidays; 156 to Littlehampton, Worthing and Brighton on the second Tuesday in the month and every Tuesday during the school holidays. Thereafter, advertised trips to the seaside were run as Excursions.

An example of the shortened Volvo B10M coach chassis, F296 RMH had a thirty-nine-seat Plaxton Paramount body. When photographed in 2005, it had been re-registered with 'cherished' mark WPF 926. (*R. Kirwin*)

FARNHAM COACHES

To the west of Guildford along the Hog's Back, lies the town of Farnham. It was here that Harry Parratt started his Petrich Coaches business in 1946. The name 'Petrich' was a combination of the abbreviated names of his two young twin sons, Peter and Richard. Harry's father, Frederick Parratt owned a substantial road haulage business and Petrich Coaches shared its Wrecclesham premises, on the south-western outskirts of Farnham on the road to Bordon. In later years, when F. W. Parratt Haulage found itself in difficulties, that business was re-constituted as Farnham Transport, with Harry, Peter and Richard as directors. In due course the coach operations were incorporated as Farnham Coaches (Petrich) Ltd.

In 1978, two employees purchased the company – Peter Collins, a driver and his wife Marjorie, who worked in the office. After the abolition of road service licensing for tours and excursions in 1980, they developed a range of holiday tours and day trips, some of which were marketed under the 'Weyside Tours' banner. In 1982 there arrived one of the first Kassbohrer Setra touring coaches in the UK, followed by several more. The workshop was available to outside customers too, as a Public Service Vehicle, Heavy Goods Vehicle and car MOT testing station.

Eventually, more than twenty vehicles were operated. However, due to doctor's advice connected with Peter's health problems that started in January 1988, he decided to sell the business, with several unacceptable offers being received in the months that followed. As no deal could be concluded, Collins decided to sell his premises and advertised the vehicles and workshop equipment separately. However, his manager talked to a number of local operators and eventually, on 1 September 1988, Safeguard acquired the goodwill and five Setra coaches. These coaches all came with 'cherished' FCG registration marks, which with the acquisition of other such marks, have been retained, being progressively transferred to later fleet additions. The other vehicles owned by Farnham Coaches were not acquired and were sold separately. Three of them passed to local operator Ray Bolton of Folly Hill, near Farnham, who employed Richard Parratt as a driver. When Bolton ceased to trade, having used the name Swiftsure Coaches (the Operating Centre was at TS Swiftsure in Badshot Lea), Richard was subsequently given a job by Safeguard at Farnham.

Five drivers and a mechanic transferred to Safeguard. As Farnham Coaches had much customer loyalty in the area, the name and the mauve,

Above left: Our first illustrative sample of the Setra coaches acquired with the Farnham Coaches business in September 1988, shows 159 FCG, a forty-seven-seat model with on-board toilet. It shows well the somewhat unusual livery inherited by Safeguard and perpetuated until 2005 on Farnham-based coaches; it also displays the Weyside Tours name originated by Peter Collins. Epsom Racecourse, 1992. (*L. Smith*)

Above right: Another Setra acquired from Peter Collins was 247 FCG, in the livery of Globus, for whom Farnham Coaches ran tours through a sub-contract arrangement with Landtourers. (*Safeguard Collection*)

Left: B906 SPR, similar to B907 SPR already encountered, was in due course transferred by Safeguard from Guildford to Farnham depot and put into a revised Farnham Coaches livery, based on the original. (*Safeguard Collection*)

purple and pink livery were perpetuated, to keep the business separate from the Guildford operations. The unusual vehicle colour scheme had originated when a coach had been purchased from Tex Tours of Bournemouth and it replaced the previous two-tone grey livery. While the business separation had some benefits, it gradually became more problematical for various reasons and less cost-effective, thus gradual integration later occurred as will be noted in due course.

After the takeover, Ken Pullen, who had been appointed as Transport Manager by Peter Collins in 1986, continued to oversee activities, including excursions, short break tours, school contracts and private hire, as well as having some coaches working under contract to Landtourer Coaches on tours for Globus Holidays in a bespoke livery. It was agreed that Safeguard could rent the original premises in Wrecclesham at 42 The Street, next to the Bear and Ragged Staff public house, for a few months. However, Peter Collins wished to sell the land for housing development, Safeguard being given one week's notice to quit in November 1988. Although the Newmans put in a bid, it was unsuccessful and it was necessary to find alternative premises very rapidly. In the short term, the only place that Ken Pullen and Gordon Button could find to base the business was on a piece of rough open ground at Hollybush Lane Industrial Estate near Aldershot, where there were no facilities whatsoever, having previously been used as a landfill site. Buckets had to be filled by hand with water from a nearby pond in order to wash the coaches.

Therefore, after an initial suggestion from Peter Parratt, Safeguard committed to a £0.5 million investment to acquire a 0.75 acre site from Will Cooper, situated on the A287 Odiham Road, near Ewshot, north of Farnham. The high cost resulted from the land already being zoned for industrial use. The coaches were moved in on Christmas Eve 1988. This was a far more suitable location and over a period of time, hard-standing was laid and an office, staff facilities, a workshop building with pits and a vehicle lift and coach washing and fuelling facilities were installed, being completed by September 1989. The new office replaced a temporary Portakabin on the site and a rented office in East Street in Farnham. The five Setra coaches were supplemented with some Leyland coaches from Guildford. The Ewshot site is just in the Hart District Council area of Hampshire, a county transferred from the South Eastern to the Western Traffic Area on 1 June 1991, so a new Operator's Licence was needed. However, officialdom took some time to catch up and a Western Traffic Area Licence was not issued until January 1996, back-dated to 1 May 1994. Also in 1991, Guildford became part of the combined South Eastern & Metropolitan Traffic Area.

Inherited by Safeguard with the Farnham Coaches takeover was an arrangement whereby Landtourer Coaches Ltd used Farnham Coaches premises as the nominated Operating Centre on its operator's licence with Ken Pullen as its Transport Manager. Formed in autumn 1984, Landtourer was the UK arm of Bernard Kavanagh & Sons Ltd of Urlingford in Eire. Landtourer's vehicles were parked at Wrecclesham (and later Ewshot) for short periods in the summer season between extended tours run by them on behalf of Globus. These inclusive tours were marketed to incoming American tourists and Kavanagh was a major contractor. Under the continuing arrangement, Safeguard undertook routine inspections and servicing on Landtourer vehicles at Ewshot, while Landtourers sub-contracted up to five coaches worth of work to Farnham Coaches. The latter therefore used its own vehicles, a number of which were to carry Globus livery and branding, with its own drivers, for an agreed daily rate.

The second half of the 1980s saw Safeguard's choice of coach turn to the Volvo B10M with Plaxton bodywork. Five such vehicles were purchased from Excelsior Coaches of Bournemouth while an example of the shortened version of this type with thirty-nine seats arrived in August

Another pair of Volvo B10M/Plaxton Paramount coaches arrived from Excelsior in autumn 1989. F475 WFX was allocated to Farnham and re-registered 196 FCG, a mark purchased to complement those acquired with the Farnham Coaches business. These 'cherished' FCG marks have been transferred several times onto different coaches, as a means to disguise their age. (*Safeguard Collection*)

By contrast, the other coach of the pair – F474 WFX – was allocated to Guildford in Safeguard livery and retained its original registration until departure in October 1998. (*K. Wheal Collection*)

Something more unusual for the Farnham-based stock, was this Taz Dubrava forty-nine-seat coach, purchased in January 1990 after use by Thandi Coaches of Bearwood, West Midlands. It was later registered DSK 558. One wonders what Bert Newman would have thought of such a foreign vehicle. (*L. Smith*)

Obviously pleased with the Volvo B10Ms purchased from Excelsior, Safeguard acquired some more. G514 EFX, parked here at Corfe Castle in Dorset in 1996, was owned from October 1990 until August 2010 and for a period carried the registration 247 FCG. (*R. Kirwin*)

1988 – F296 RMH. This was to be the last new coach until 1996. Bedford coaches had almost been removed from the fleet by the end of the decade, while the last bus from this manufacturer, TPL 166S, departed in July 1987. In 1987/88, four of the new forty-nine-seat Leyland Lynx buses (D165 HML, E51 MMT and E297/8 OMG) were purchased to replace some of the Leyland Leopards, becoming front-line performers on the main Guildford town services. The Lynx was far more technically-advanced and complex compared to the well-tried Leopard, but an important advantage was a much lower step height. Ken Newman suggested that if a low-floor Leopard had been available, Safeguard would have bought them.

In readiness for privatisation, the 'southern' part of Alder Valley became, appropriately, Alder Valley South Ltd on 1 January 1986. Sold to Frontsource Ltd, owned by Robert Beattie, in November 1987, it was sold to Q-Drive Ltd just a year later. When one of Q-Drive's directors wished to leave the business, it was found necessary to raise funds by selling Alder Valley operations based on Guildford, Cranleigh and Woking. The buyer, on 15 December 1990, was Drawlane PLC, which already owned neighbouring London Country Bus (South West) Ltd. A company called Randomquick Ltd was used for the acquisition and this traded as Alder Valley West Surrey, being controlled by the London Country management team.

Some of Safeguard's less well-used services began to require outside financial assistance if they were to continue. The G9/10 services to the Northway and Foxburrows area received top-up funding from Surrey County Council from July 1988, through a mechanism known in the trade as a 'Deminimis Agreement'. This was followed by similar support for the Sunday buses on G4 from January 1991 and the evening service from September 1992.

A somewhat less-successful venture was a commuter coach service to Hammersmith, in London, from Alton and Farnham that was operated

Farnham Coaches had this impressive MCW Metroliner double deck coach on loan in early 1991 for their short-lived and unsuccessful experimental commuter service to London. Even the slogan 'London in Comfort' did not tempt enough people away from their car and/or rail journey. (*G. Button Collection*)

The development of new services in Guildford, covering areas unsuitable for Safeguard's normal full-size buses, meant the need for additional smaller vehicles. D633 XVV was an early Optare product, known as the City Pacer, from the days before that manufacturer became dominant in the Safeguard bus fleet. On a Volkswagen LT55 chassis, this twenty-five-seater was used for five years after acquisition from Leicester Citybus in June 1991. (*Safeguard Collection*)

Kit and Bernard Newman. (*Newman Family Collection*)

by Farnham Coaches as a trial from 7 – 18 January 1991. Marketed as 'London in Comfort', a Metro Cammell Metroliner double deck coach registered D192 ESC was hired from Kavanagh's to run it. With two journeys each way during peak hours on Mondays to Fridays, the fares were £8.50 day return and £35 for a weekly ticket – considerably less than the comparable rail fares. However, fewer than five people used it on average and the service failed to catch the public's interest, to Ken Pullen's disappointment; it soon ceased and the vehicle left the fleet.

Bernard Newman 'retired' from full-time employment with the company on 30 June 1990 and became the Non-Executive Chairman.

SAFEGUARD
Tours 88

DAY EXCURSIONS AND TOURS

TEL: GUILDFORD 61103 / 573215

'BUS WARS' OF THE 1990s

As well as losing some Surrey County Council contracts and gaining a few more for generally short periods, the 1990s were marked by significant new bus service competition for Safeguard in its Guildford heartland. In April 1991, the main Park Barn services were re-organised on weekdays to operate in a circular fashion – G4 out of town via Woodbridge Road, Aldershot Road and Southway, returning via the hospital and Guildford Park, with G5 undertaking the reverse. On Sundays, the half-hourly G4 ran both ways via its traditional route. From 2 September 1991, Alder Valley West Surrey diverted part of its Woking–Guildford via Pirbright and Worplesdon service 28 to also serve Fairlands, Wood Street Green, Park Barn Drive and Guildford Park (ostensibly to serve the hospital), renumbering these journeys as 28B. Although this only lasted about four months, Alder Valley West Surrey, by now renamed Guildford & West Surrey Buses Ltd (G&WS) returned in force on 14 March 1992, when the Guildford town services saw a major re-organisation which made them strongly competitive towards Safeguard. Their services 16/17 serving Rydes Hill, Fairlands and Wood Street and 26/27 covering Stoughton and Grange Park, also ran via Guildford Park, the hospital, Park Barn shops and the western part of Cabell Road. Those areas were also served by a service 37 out to Fairlands Estate. This resulted in four G&WS buses per hour between the town centre and Park Barn, which combined with Safeguard's services, meant that the far end of Park Barn was experiencing around fifteen bus movements each hour. These actions followed an interesting suggestion made by G&WS that Safeguard should run their buses under a franchise agreement with G&WS, being paid an agreed rate for this, with revenue going to the larger concern. The answer from Safeguard was a rapid refusal.

This over-provision in excess of demand made little commercial sense and prompted further discussions between the players. Another re-structure of G&WS services on 29 August 1992 saw them removed from the west end of Southway, Cabell Road and Barnwood Road, running instead via the whole length of Park Barn Drive, similar to Blue Saloon's G2 service, at twenty minute intervals. Service 27 also served the Northway area on a commercial basis, from which Safeguard withdrew again as the Council now had no need to subsidise it.

More bad news for Safeguard followed, as it was unsuccessful in retaining the substantial contract for service 550 Aldershot-Camberley,

Popular for small coaches in the 1980s were Toyota HB31Rs with Portuguese bodywork by Caetano, marketed in the UK through the Moseley dealership. Safeguard acquired this twenty-one-seat example of the Optimo model in August 1992, registered H672 ATN. (*R. Kirwin*)

In June 1993, there was a return to the Safeguard fleet of a bus chassis made locally in Guildford. K628 YPL was a ubiquitous Dennis Dart with Plaxton Pointer body, seen in summer 1994 while operating on service G12 in Merrow's Bushy Hill estate, an area to the east of Guildford into which Safeguard expanded largely in retaliation for competitive incursions by London & Country/Guildford & West Surrey into Park Barn. (*Author's Collection*)

SAFEGUARD Coaches

514

Your new bus service linking Heath End, Weybourne and Shortheath with Farnham Town Centre from 4th October 1993

- Introducing a handy new link from residential areas in Heath End and Weybourne to Farnham on Mondays to Fridays

- "Hail & Ride" service along South Avenue, West Avenue, North Avenue, Upper Weybourne Lane, Newcome Road, Courtenay Road, Knights Road and Brooklands Road. Buses will stop on request at any safe point

- More buses into Farnham from Burnt Hill Road, Lodge Hill Road and Abbot's Ride

- Serving the new Sainsburys in Water Lane when store opens in December

This is an experimental service provided by Surrey County Council. Its long term future will depend on the amount of support it receives.

Full details of times shown overleaf

For further information contact:
Safeguard Coaches Ltd, Friary Bus Station, Guildford, Surrey
Tel: Guildford 61103

SURREY COUNTY COUNCIL

Above: Twenty-nine-seat Mercedes Benz/Optare Star Rider G122 KUB entered the Farnham Coaches fleet in 1993 and was previously owned by Brents of Watford. (*Safeguard Collection*)

Left: A leaflet produced by Surrey County Council to promote short-lived contracted service 514 around Farnham, serving residential areas away from regular bus services.

Above left: A second Dennis Dart/Plaxton Pointer arrived in January 1994. L265 EPD is turning into Guildford Park Road, en-route to Park Barn on service 5 in August 1998. (*R. Kirwin*)

Above right:This Mercedes Benz 609D with twenty-four-seat body by Made to Measure, performed in the 1990s on Safeguard's 'secondary' network of Guildford town services, in this case on service 11 to the Merrow area in July 1995. (*R. Kirwin*)

Left: Safeguard has accreditation from an organisation known as BUSK – 'Belt Up School Kids' – which exists to promote good practice and to improve safety for children when travelling to or from school by bus or coach.

which after 29 August 1992, was awarded to the remaining part of Alder Valley Ltd owned by Q-Drive. However, a new contract was gained from 4 October 1993 for a service 514 on Mondays to Fridays, linking Farnham with residential areas in south Farnham, The Bourne, Shortheath, Heath End and Weybourne, also serving the Sainsbury store in Water Lane. Aimed primarily at shoppers and usually operated with an Optare City Pacer or Optare Star Rider midibus, the contract for this service passed to Frimley Coaches at the end of May 1994.

The contract to provide service 559, by then renumbered 659, to Bishop David Brown School from Byfleet was regained in September 1994, having been lost to London & Country in July 1992, while another contract gain was a new service 686 from the area south of Woking to George Abbot School in Burpham. At the same time, predatory competition from G&WS escalated again when the latter started service 14 every twenty minutes from the town centre to Park Barn Shops via Aldershot Road, Southway and Cabell Road, running just a few minutes in front of Safeguard's G4. This may well have been a response to Safeguard expanding into the area east of Guildford to Bushy Hill in Merrow, competing with Guildford & West Surrey. New Safeguard services commenced on 15 August 1994, once per hour on each of G11 via Tormead Road, Boxgrove Lane and Merrow Woods and G12 via London Road. These did newly serve some areas not covered by G&WS, but the latter regarded Bushy Hill as their own domain. Two months later, the G11 was diverted to include Sheeplands Avenue in Bushy Hill Estate and G12 altered to run direct along the Epsom Road, five minutes in front of G&WS service 8.

Despite the arrival of G&WS in Park Barn, many residents remained loyal to Safeguard. A number of letters to the Surrey Advertiser followed. One suggested that 'Safeguard without having any divine right to serve us, has performed the task so well over so many years that many people must feel that they have an absolute right to serve the area. I almost feel like yelling Come on you Reds'. However, those sentiments were contrary to the free market spirit of enterprise promoted by Nicholas Ridley MP, the architect of the Transport Act 1985, although it is questionable whether competitive choice was either sustainable or necessary in a town like Guildford. Safeguard wrote a plainly-worded letter registering their concerns on 'David versus Goliath' competition to local MP David Howell, receiving only a factual reply, promising little.

With such a volatile situation with little commercial benefit, negotiations were held in November 1994 after G&WS had registered revised timings on the 3 to Bellfields just in front of the Safeguard journeys. Initially G&WS proposed that Safeguard hand over the entire G4 service but sufficient conciliation was achieved to allow further changes as soon as 28 January 1995, after Safeguard had even privately considered selling the bus operations to the larger concern. Safeguard G12 along Epsom Road was withdrawn while G&WS abandoned service 14, having reached agreement with Safeguard to share the operation of twenty-minute interval service G4 on Mondays to Saturdays, although G&WS did not use the 'G' number prefix. Each operator supplied one vehicle. This was on a similar basis to that which continued to apply on service 3 to Bellfields. While there was still some overlap, it was the end of openly predatory competition between G&WS and Safeguard around Guildford.

Blue Saloon decided they would like some more Park Barn traffic from September 1995, when they diverted their service G2 to cover the west end of Southway and Cabell Road. This was fairly short-lived as Blue Saloon's services were acquired in March 1996 by British Bus PLC (re-named from Drawlane Group in 1992), the parent of G&WS. The former Blue Saloon services were quickly assimilated into the G&WS Guildford town network, with the G2 withdrawn from 9 April as an amended G&WS 27 was used to cover much of the ground, but not including the west end of Park Barn. There then ensued a much-needed period of relative stability.

Above left: A pair of Volvo B10M/Plaxton Premiere coaches arrived from Wallace Arnold of Leeds in 1995. J745 CWT was later registered DSK 558 but had been changed back to its original mark ready for its departure from Guildford on 13 February 2003. (*Safeguard Collection*)

Above right: A Volvo B10M bought new in February 1996 (N561 UPF) was later registered 531 FCG, as seen here in September 2005 on a private hire at Tonbridge School. By then, Safeguard livery was becoming standard on Farnham Coaches vehicles, although the latter name was retained. (*R. Kirwin*)

Left: Mercedes Benz 814D/Plaxton Beaver M295 THD is parked at Crowthorne station, during a private hire for Charterhouse School in Godalming, to Wellington College, for a sports fixture. (*R. Kirwin*)

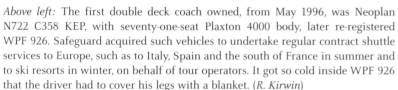

Above left: The first double deck coach owned, from May 1996, was Neoplan N722 C358 KEP, with seventy-one-seat Plaxton 4000 body, later re-registered WPF 926. Safeguard acquired such vehicles to undertake regular contract shuttle services to Europe, such as to Italy, Spain and the south of France in summer and to ski resorts in winter, on behalf of tour operators. It got so cold inside WPF 926 that the driver had to cover his legs with a blanket. (*R. Kirwin*)

Above right: Parked in Guildford bus station was Dennis Javelin/Plaxton Paramount J807 FNJ. On the left is Ian Northrup and Malcolm Toghill stands on the right at the front; he has worked for Safeguard since 1986, with a short break. (*Safeguard Collection*)

Right: Unlike G122 KUB featured earlier, similar Optare Star Rider G89KUB was a disliked bus once owned by London operator Metroline. Purchased in December 1996, here it is leaving the yard 'hopefully for the last time', John Lake at the wheel, en route to dealer Mike Nash: September 2002. (*Safeguard Collection*)

The first of many Van Hool – bodied coaches for Safeguard was P46 GPG, later DSK 559, new in February 1997 on a Volvo B10M chassis. Graham Newman visited the Van Hool factory in Belgium in connection with its purchase and it is still in the fleet, being a much-liked vehicle which currently has the most longevity in terms of ownership. (*R. Kirwin*)

To maintain its position as a leading local coach operator, Safeguard always moves with the times. The argument over the safety benefits of fitting seat belts in coaches was receiving some national press coverage, especially where school children were being carried. Therefore, the Safeguard coach fleet was equipped with seat belts in 1994, being one of the first firms in Surrey to do so.

Ken Newman's son David, who as previously mentioned made his career as an antique dealer and furniture restorer, living in Oxfordshire, joined the Board as a Director in March 1995, as did Graham Newman.

Consequent to a revision to Stagecoach Hants & Surrey's (who had acquired the remainder of Alder Valley in October 1992) commercial and contracted services around Farnham, Safeguard gained a Surrey County

Council contract to run service 16 from 6 January to 3 May 1997, after which it was contracted to Tillingbourne Bus Co. in a revised form. This linked Dockenfield with Farnham via Rowledge, Shortheath and Menin Way, continuing across Farnham to the Sainsbury store. 1997 ended with Safeguard running two Christmas season Park and Ride services into Guildford for a few weeks – the 102 from George Abbot School and the 103 from a car park at the University of Surrey. Funded by the Borough Council, they were intended to relieve pressure on town centre car parks in the Christmas shopping and New Year Sales periods.

Having purchased British Bus PLC in June 1996, Cowie PLC was subsequently re-constituted as Arriva. Operations from the Guildford depot in Leas Road, together with its Cranleigh outstation were put into the name of Arriva Guildford & West Surrey Ltd from 29 June 1998. Just under a month later there were major changes made to Arriva services in Surrey. These included the cessation of the Guildford to Boxgrove Park section of service 1 and the withdrawal of services 14 to Northway and 18 to Charlotteville. As replacement, the County Council awarded Deminimis Agreements to Safeguard to operate service 10 from the town centre to Charlotteville, Warren Road and Boxgrove Park and a limited service 14 from Northway to town via Woodside Road, Foxburrows Avenue, Park Barn Drive, the hospital and Guildford Park. The latter only lasted until 28 November that year and removed Safeguard from the Northway area. Also, Safeguard finally dropped the 'G' prefix from the service 3, 4 and 5 numbers.

Evolution of the Safeguard and Farnham Coaches fleets in the 1990s was somewhat similar to that of many other operators, where foreign manufacturers started to predominate. On the coach side, more Volvo B10Ms and Setras were acquired, but also some Dennis Javelins as well as examples of the Neoplan Skyliner, MCW Metroliner and a Taz Dubrava. Most of the more exotic vehicles were in the Farnham Coaches fleet. The

Above: Jane and Graham Newman with grandson James.
(*Newman Family Collection*)

Right: August 1997 timetable for G5 and G11 routes.

G5 — BUS STATION – RSC Hospital – PARK BARN ESTATE – Woodbridge Hill – BUS STATION

Monday to Saturdays

						B						
GUILDFORD Friary Bus Station	–	–	0655*	0715	Then at	35	55	15		1755	–	–	–	1855
Guildford Park, The Chase	–	–	0701*	0721	these	41	01	21	until	1801	–	–	–	1901
RSC Hospital	–	–	7005*	0725	mins past	45	05	25		1805	–	–	–	1905
Cabell Rd/Park Barn Drive	0630	0650	0708	0728	each hour	48	08	28		1808	1818	1838	1858	1908
Park Barn Shops	0633	0653	0713	0733		53	13	33		1813	1823	1843	1903	1913
Southway P.O.	0638	0658	0718	0738		58	18	38		1818	1828	1848	1908	–
Woodbridge Hill	0640	0700	0720	0740		00	20	40		1820	1830	1850	1910	–
GUILDFORD Friary Bus Station	0646	0706	0726	0746		06	26	46		1826	1836	1856	1916	–

Joint service with Guildford & West Surrey.

CODES:
* – Not Saturdays.
B – Journeys from 0915 until 1715 run via Park Barn Drive and Barnwood Road to rejoin Cabell Road at the Youth Centre.

G11 — RSC Hospital – GUILDFORD – Boxgrove Park – BUSHY HILL

Monday to Saturdays

	NS	NS						NS	NS	NS	NS	NS
RSC Hospital	–	0805	–	–	1030	1130	1230	1330	1430	1530	1630	1730
Tesco Superstore	–	–	–	–	1032	1132	–	1332	1432	1532	1632	1732
Guildford Park, Chase	–	0808	–	–	1035	1135	1235	1335	1435	1535	1635	1735
GUILDFORD, Friary (Bay 16)	–	0815	0845	0945	1045	1145	1245	1345	1445	1545	1645	1745
London Road Station	–	0820	0850	0949	1049	1149	1249	1349	1449	1549	1649	1749
Tormead Road	–	0824	0854	0952	1052	1152	1252	1352	1452	1552	1652	1752
Boxgrove Park, Collingwood	–	0827	0857	0955	1055	1155	1255	1355	1455	1555	1655	1755
Bushy Hill, Longdyke	–	0830	0900	0958	1058	1158	1258	1358	1458	1558	1658	1758
dep.	0740	0830	0900	1000	1100	1200	1300	1400	1500	1600	1700	–
Boxgrove Park, Collingwood	0744	0834	0904	1004	1104	12004	1304	1404	1504	1604	1704	–
Tormead Road	0747	0837	0907	1007	1107	1207	1307	1407	1507	1607	1707	–
London Road Station	0749	0839	0909	1009	1109	1209	1309	1409	1509	1609	1709	–
GUILDFORD, Friary	0754	0844	0914	1014	1114	1214	1314	1414	1514	1614	1714	–
(Bay 13) dep.	–	–	–	1020	1120	1220	1320*	1420	1520	1620	1720	–
Guildford Park, Chase	–	–	–	1026	1126	1226	1326*	1426	1526	1626	1726	–
Tesco Superstore	–	–	–	1028	1128	–	1328*	1428	1528	1628		–
RSC Hospital	–	–	–	1030	1130	1230	1330*	1430	1530	1630	1730	–

Also calls at Research Park, Gill Ave at 1231, 1331 and 1731.

CODES:
* or NS – NOT Saturdays.

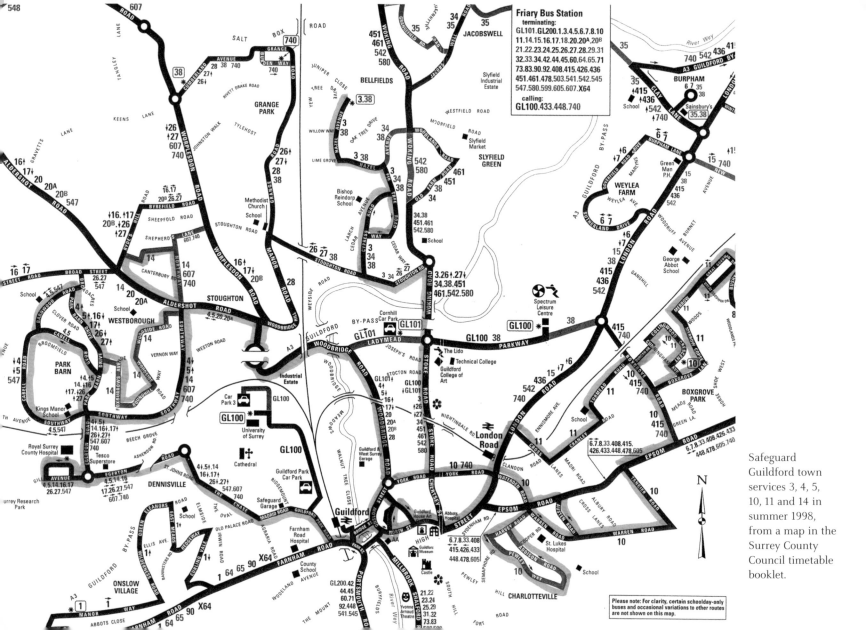

Safeguard Guildford town services 3, 4, 5, 10, 11 and 14 in summer 1998, from a map in the Surrey County Council timetable booklet.

Above left: In March 1997, four EOS E180Z coaches (M622-5 RCP) were acquired from Landtourers for Farnham Coaches. They were in Globus livery and already based at Ewshot and were given FCG cherished registrations, such as 196 FCG seen here, previously M623 RCP, which was owned until December 2005. It is depicted in September 2005, wearing Farnham Coaches colours (*R. Kirwin*)

Above right: MCW Metroliner tri-axle double deck coach MIW 8529 was a second-hand acquisition, caught by the camera while in plain white livery. On ski resort shuttle work, such vehicles were found to have poor braking on the steep alpine roads and were prone to overheating. (*Safeguard Collection*)

Right: Posed in the yard at Ridgemount by Richard Kirwin, L967 RUB was another Toyota/Caetano Optimo and was previously owned by Applegates of Newport, Gloucs. It had originated with Wallace Arnold Tours. It is located roughly where Brickyard Cottage once stood. (*R. Kirwin*)

Above left: Still presently owned is fifty-seven-seat Dennis Javelin/Plaxton Premiere S503 UAK, photographed at Swanage. It shows off well the Safeguard livery style applied to coaches purchased 1986–2005. (*R. Kirwin*)

Above right: One of two Dennis Darts with Northern Counties bodywork acquired from a leasing company in September 1998 in order to replace two Leyland Lynx. (*K. Wheal Collection*)

Below left: The other Dennis Dart/Northern Counties (M388 KVR) is on service 4 in Park Barn. This one was replaced by a new Optare Tempo in April 2006. (*R. Kirwin*)

Below right: This impressive Neoplan Skyliner came in October 1998 as F617 CWJ, being re-registered XHY 378. In 2001 it is at Tonbridge School, with WPF 926 just visible behind it. This vehicle replaced a previous Neoplan (also XHY 378 but sold as A385 XGG) which had lasted about a year and was somewhat unreliable, having had eight owners before Safeguard and at least four afterwards. (*R. Kirwin*)

majority of these acquisitions were pre-owned, including four EOS E180Z coaches previously owned by Bernard Kavanagh of Urlingford in Eire, which arrived in March 1997. Initially, the latter continued to be used in the white Globus livery on touring work under contract to Landtourers. However, new purchases consisted of a pair of Plaxton Premiere-bodied coaches, one a Dennis Javelin and one a Volvo B10M in February 1996 (N561/2 UPF), a Volvo B10M/Van Hool (P46 GPG) a year later and another Javelin/Plaxton Premiere (S503 UAK) in August 1998.

For the bus fleet, the 1990s saw the advent of the ubiquitous Dennis Dart; two new examples with forty-seat Plaxton Pointer bodywork (K628 YPL and L265 EPD) came in 1993/4, while two pre-owned Darts with Northern Counties bodywork came in September 1998. Smaller buses for use on the 'back road' services included a Mercedes Benz 609D twenty-four-seater (F623 FNA) and a twenty-nine-seat Mercedes 811D/Optare Star Rider (G89 KUB). The last pair of Leopard/Duple Dominant buses departed in February 1994, while two similar Leyland Tigers lasted until November 2001. The four Lynx left the fleet in 1996 and 1998.

Although 'Deregulation' had prompted new bus service opportunities, patronage had inexorably declined since the 'golden years' of the late 1940s/early 1950s. Over a long period, bus service revenue for Safeguard has become subsidiary to that gained from private hire, contract work and touring. It is perhaps worthwhile to illustrate patronage by a few snapshots. In 1955, 2,385,000 passenger journeys were made on the Safeguard bus services, with mileage operated being 247,560. By 1969, these figures had reduced to 2,003,000 and 242,271 respectively. However, the 1970s onwards witnessed an acceleration of the decline such that in the 1998/1999 financial year, Safeguard recorded 798,000 passenger journeys with a mileage of 213,685. Little explanation is needed regarding the changing socio-economic circumstances that brought about this drop in ridership over the last fifty years or so.

In December 1999, the Newman family celebrated the 100th birthday of Ethel Newman, Bert's widow, at Ashley House in Shalford. Standing at the rear, left to right are Barnaby, David, Graham and Mark while left to right at the front are Bern, Ethel (with James) and Ken. (*Newman Family Collection*)

THE NEW MILLENNIUM

The end of the 1990s saw the start of work which led to a substantial contract for the University of Surrey from December 2000, under the auspices of the European Institute of Health & Medical Sciences. This required three or four coaches each day to transport student nurses to and from hospitals as far afield as Chichester, Crawley, Redhill, Frimley and Basingstoke. This could be integrated in a cost-effective way with school contracts and operated for forty-eight weeks per year. However, the company's largest customer was the Royal Grammar School in Guildford, for the provision of transport from its town centre site to the playing fields at Shalford, some distance away and the transport of sports teams to 'away' fixtures.

The first year of the New Millennium saw the arrival of Andrew Halliday, who had previously worked for London Buses and the MVA Consultancy, which was a prelude to the retirement of Gordon Button as Company Secretary and Traffic Manager in April 2001. Ken Newman passed away in late May 2001 and his shareholding transferred to his widow, Gill, who later became a Director.

On 4 September 2000, Safeguard commenced running a free regular shuttle bus service around Guildford town centre, under contract to the Borough Council. This was intended to help stimulate shopping activity at the top end of the steeply-inclined High Street and North Street, being part of the town's Transport Strategy; it became a useful facility, especially for the less-mobile. It ran in a circuit from the Friary Bus Station and the rail station via seven other stops in the High Street, Sydenham Road, Epsom Road and North Street, every fifteen minutes with two buses (later reduced to every twenty minutes with one bus in September 2001) on Mondays to Saturdays. Two pre-owned twenty-nine-seat Dennis Dart/Plaxton Pointer buses were rented for the service (V943/6 DNB), the first easy access buses for Safeguard. The Guildford Shuttle was sufficiently successful for the contract to be extended beyond its initial six month term.

Guildford Borough Council favoured the use of an Optare Alero minibus on the Town Shuttle service, so one was ordered by Safeguard. Originally expected in September 2001, it was delayed by four months, YL51 ZTK arriving in January 2002 to replace the remaining leased Mini Pointer Dart. However, the Alero proved inadequate in terms of its manual transmission and capacity, as the Shuttle was carrying 1,500

Above left: A short 8.5m Dennis Dart was purchased in January 2000, for use on secondary bus duties. H577 MOC had a Carlyle body which had been rebuilt by a bus dealership called Fleetmaster, with a Plaxton Pointer front and badged as a Dartline. In 2001, it is turning from Guildford's Upper High Street into North Street on its way back from Merrow on service 10, the contract for which Safeguard lost to Countryliner in September 2002. (*R. Kirwin*)

Above right: DSK 559 was a one-off as far as Safeguard was concerned. Originally registered P970 HWF, it was a Dennis Javelin with Neoplan Transliner bodywork, previously owned by Busbridge of Ashford, Kent. It was known by the staff as the 'Solar Polar' as a consequence of its previous owner's livery depicting a polar bear. Despite this nickname, its air conditioning was ineffective and the coach was much disliked by engineers and drivers. (*PM Photography*)

Right: For the launch of Guildford Town Shuttle service in 2000, two low floor twenty-nine-seat Dennis Darts with Plaxton's Mini Pointer bodywork were leased from a dealer and put into the special livery shown here. They were the largest vehicles that could negotiate a particularly tight corner on the route and V946 DNB seen here lasted the longer of the two, being replaced by an Optare Alero minibus. (*Author*)

This former Flights of Birmingham Dennis Javelin/Plaxton Premiere arrived in December 2000 and is seen in October 2002 parked adjacent to Southsea Castle. (*R. Kirwin*)

passengers a week, so it was replaced by another (new) low floor Dart/Plaxton Pointer VU02 TTJ as soon as April 2002. This vehicle was of the maximum length (8.5m) that could be safely used on the service, due to a particularly tight corner.

In March 2001, the substantial, much-respected and lamented Tillingbourne Bus Co. unexpectedly went into receivership and closed down overnight. Its final fleet included two low-floor Optare Excel buses (X307/8 CBT) and six months later Safeguard was able to purchase these as replacements for the last two Leyland Tiger/Duple Dominant buses. This saw the start of a relationship with Optare which has seen virtually all investment in new buses placed with the Leeds-based firm, rather

than with the local firm of Dennis. Originally the Excels operated two of the three duties on routes 4 and 5 and apparently patronage increased by nearly 8 per cent within the first year. A new Excel (YJ03 UMM) was then purchased from dealer stock in April 2003, to allow service 3 to Bellfields to benefit from an easy access bus.

Safeguard vacated their office in Guildford's Friary Bus Station in August 2001, with its functions transferred to the premises at Ridgemount, so all activities in the town were concentrated on one site for the first time. By then, Safeguard had an annual turnover of £2.5 million; 75 per cent was generated by the seventeen coaches based at Guildford and the fourteen which were operated by Farnham Coaches. The nine buses accounted for the remainder.

From 27 January 2001, service 10 had been extended from Boxgrove Park to Merrow (Great Goodwin Drive), to complement service 11. However, the County Council subsidy required for the 10/11 had increased to the point where a re-tendering exercise was thought prudent and unfortunately the resulting contract was lost to Countryliner, another locally based concern, from 2 September 2002. On Safeguard's last day, a special vehicle was used, driven by Alan Belcher. As previously mentioned, several Safeguard vehicles migrated to Somerset following purchase by Safeway Services of South Petherton. One of these was AEC Reliance/Burlingham bus 200 APB of 1956, which then passed into preservation and most interestingly was re-purchased by Safeguard in January 2002 from Stephen Morris' Rexquote fleet at Bishops Lydeard. Although it was expected to pay its way as an option for wedding and corporate specialist hire, it is also a good public relations tool for special occasions.

The whole coach transport requirement for the XVII Commonwealth Games shooting events held at Bisley was provided by the Safeguard/Farnham Coaches fleet in July/August 2002. The competitors and officials were accommodated at the University of Surrey in Guildford; the work

Above left: Acquired for Globus contract tour operation by Farnham Coaches, Y161/2 HWE were MAN 18.350s with Neoplan Transliner bodywork, carrying bespoke Globus livery initially. Globus work finished at the end of the 2005 season but these coaches were not sold until 2007. (*L. Smith*)

Above right: In April 2001, Gordon Button retired after around thirty-two years service to Safeguard, as Traffic Manager and Company Secretary. On that occasion we see, left to right, Graham Newman, Bern Newman, Gordon and Ken Newman. (*Safeguard Collection*)

Right: When Tillingbourne Bus Co. of Cranleigh sadly and catastrophically collapsed in March 2001, several of their modern vehicles were sold by dealers to new owners. Safeguard acquired two Optare Excels in September 2001 which were then barely one year old. This started a relationship with Optare which has led to a standardisation on that make for the main bus fleet. Apart from the leased Shuttle vehicles, these Excels were the first Safeguard low floor easy-access buses. They were painted in coach livery, as have been all subsequent new buses. X307 CBT is in Hazel Avenue in Bellfields Estate on service 3 in May 2010. (*R. Kirwin*)

included timetabled shuttle services from Guildford to Bisley and to Reading Station for train connections to the main Games venue at Manchester, as well as transfers to and from Heathrow Airport and an internal shuttle service at Bisley Ranges. At the other end of the scale, Safeguard came to the short term emergency aid of Surrey County Council when it needed a replacement operator at short notice for a group of infrequent school and shoppers contracted bus services in rural areas of west Surrey. Stagecoach resigned from the contracts at a time when it was experiencing a severe shortage of drivers. Starting on 16 September 2002, there were morning and afternoon journeys on services 688 and 698 to Waverley Abbey School at Tilford, near Farnham, interspersed by a batch of off-peak shoppers services (29, 38, 534, 535, 546, 547, 548, 549 and 565) running from various villages and residential areas into Guildford, Farnham, Burpham Sainsburys or Woking, with one journey each way, mainly on two days per week. Two vehicles were needed, providing work for those potentially surplus following the loss of the 10/11 and also school services 686 and 699. This short term contract continued until the Council was able to re-tender the work which passed in a revised form to Countryliner and Thames Bus from 13 January 2003.

Volvo B10M/Plaxton coach T530 EUB purchased in February 2003 spent five seasons from summer that year working under contract to David Urquhart Holidays on extended tours, being liveried and lettered for that company, until such activities were found to be insufficiently remunerative.

Safeguard's controlling family endured further sadness in August 2003 with the tragic passing at the early age of fifty-two of Graham Newman. While his funeral service was in progress on 19 August, Safeguard's bus services were suspended as a mark of respect. He was Company Chairman and subsequently, management of the businesses became largely the responsibility of his son Mark Graham Newman,

born in 1974 and Andrew Halliday, who hold directorships. Graham Newman's widow, Jane, continued to undertake office administration for Farnham Coaches at Ewshot and inherited his shareholding. At the same time, Bern's wife Catherine (Kit) became a shareholder and director to represent her husband's interests as he was indisposed through illness, Chris West was appointed as Operations Manager at Guildford, while Derek Holland brought long experience of coaching to a supporting office role, effectively replacing Malcolm Toghill who returned to driving coaches. Mark Newman had worked for the company for some time, before leaving and then rejoining in October 2001, taking a role on the engineering side of the business from August 2002.

Further change had come to the Park Barn services 4 and 5 on 26 July 2003, when those journeys provided by both Safeguard and Arriva which served Park Barn Drive and Barnwood Road were altered to adhere to the standard route along the length of Cabell Road. Subsequently, the evening service on route 4 passed to Arriva from 10 January 2004, together with the Council subsidy. Safeguard felt it had to resign from this contract as it was finding it difficult to obtain drivers willing to work 'antisocial' hours and it allowed a more attractive recruitment offer to be made.

The company's eightieth anniversary occurred in 2004. This was marked on 2 April by a celebratory buffet at the Holiday Inn in Guildford, where Chris Heaps, Traffic Commissioner for the South Eastern & Metropolitan Area was Guest of Honour. A portrait of the company appeared in *Buses* magazine and a limited edition model AEC Regal bus in Safeguard livery was produced by Lledo. On the same day and the day after, the vintage AEC Reliance 200 APB was used on selected journeys on services 3, 4 and 5. One of the drivers was Les Ball who joined Safeguard on a part-time basis back in 1967 and whose father and mother had also served the company for fourteen and twenty-one years respectively. His wife Betty reprised her former role as conductress from 1968 to 1981, using a manual

Above left: Two twenty-nine-seat Mercedes Benz 0814Ds with Plaxton Cheetah coach bodies, previously owned by the National Express Group for airport shuttle work were purchased in 2001 for Safeguard and 2003 for Farnham Coaches – W203 YAP and W209 YAP respectively. The former was sold in July 2013, the last coach with less than thirty-six seats. (*Safeguard Collection*)

Above right: The last double deck coach owned to date by Safeguard and in the fleet for just under three years, was Neoplan Skyliner FXU 355. Its last owner, prior to meeting its end in a Barnsley scrap yard in 2011, was 'Bound for Heaven', presumably a religious group. (*R. Kirwin*)

Right: 1956 AEC Reliance 200 APB has nostalgically returned to its origins. Having left Guildford for Safeway Services in Somerset in 1961, it had several owners after Vera Gunn sold it in 1982. Safeguard repurchased it in January 2002 for use as a promotional tool and for special occasion private hire. It was used to mark the last day of service 10 to Merrow in August 2002 and Andrew Halliday is seen with some slightly surprised customers who are boarding at Boxgrove Park. (*Author*)

Above left: Guildford Borough Council favoured the use of an Optare Alero on the Town Shuttle, which seemed like a good idea at the time but it turned out to be lacking in terms of its transmission system and inadequate capacity for demand – it only had twelve seats. YL51 ZTK arrived four months late and lasted just five months. (*A. Conway*)

Above right: This former Wallace Arnold Volvo B10M was originally registered J705 CWT, but shown here carrying 196 FCG. It was allocated to Farnham Coaches and given Globus livery for touring work. (*L. Smith*)

Left: Replacing the unsatisfactory Optare Alero on the Guildford Town Shuttle, a new Dennis Dart SLF/Plaxton Pointer was acquired in June 2002. When the Shuttle contract ended, VU02 TTJ was put onto other bus service work but between January 2009 and May 2010 it returned to the Shuttle which Safeguard re-introduced commercially, being named 'Honorary Freeman Bill Bellerby', who had strongly lead the campaign for reinstatement of the service. (*R. Kirwin*)

Above left: Volvo B10M/Van Hool S132 PGB (later WPF 926), formerly operated by Clyde Coast of Ardrossan, was captured in 2005 while undertaking touring work on behalf of David Urquhart Travel (*R. Kirwin*)

Above right: As part of the David Urquhart Tours work contracted to Safeguard, Volvo B10M/Plaxton Premiere T530 EUB was painted in a bespoke livery for five seasons up to 2008, but still remains in the fleet in standard livery. (*R. Kirwin*)

Right: With its seventy seats being especially useful for schools work, this Dennis Javelin with Plaxton's Profile bodywork was purchased new in March 2003. When photographed in June 2006 it had taken a party of Cub Scouts from Odiham to Gilwell Park in Essex. (*R. Kirwin*)

Setright ticket machine. Les found the old AEC somewhat challenging, with its heavy steering and clutch, having become used to driving more modern vehicles.

Ken Pullen retired from Farnham Coaches in April 2004, after which control of activities there was vested in Mark Newman, allowing a number of beneficial operational and administrative changes to be made and the introduction of some management systems and accounting tools already in use at Guildford. The departure of Ken Pullen coincided with the transfer of Landtourers' Operating Centre to premises in Fareham, Hampshire. There had been a decline in Globus work for Landtourers, which had seen its business reduce gradually over a few years as less American visitors came to Britain, dissuaded by terrorist threats and Foot and Mouth disease outbreaks.

By 2006, the fleet strength had contracted to thirty-five. Seven were buses (three Optare Excel, one Optare Tempo – the first bus in the fleet with an electronic destination display, one Dennis Dart SLF and two step-entrance Darts), while there were sixteen coaches at Guildford, comprising ten Volvos with either Plaxton or Van Hool bodywork, a Mercedes 0404/Hispano Vita, two Dennis Javelin/Plaxton, a seventy-seat Javelin/Plaxton and two Mercedes 0814/Plaxton Cheetah midicoaches. There was also the 1956 AEC Reliance. The Farnham Coaches fleet was made up of five Plaxton-bodied Volvos, four Setras and two MAN 18.350/Neoplan Transliner.

The purple-based livery for Farnham Coaches was disappearing in favour of the standard cream and red Safeguard coach colour scheme, although retaining Farnham Coaches fleet names, a process properly

SAFEGUARD Coaches Limited

CONTINENTAL & BRITISH EXTENDED TOURS

THE FRIARY BUS STATION · GUILDFORD · SURREY · GU1 4BB

Telephone: (01483) 61103 & 573215 Fax: (01483) 455865

Left: To allow for the Bellfields service to be operated by a low floor bus, a new Optare Excel was delivered in April 2003, to facilitate transfer of another vehicle from services 4 and 5 to service 3. In this view, the Excel is near Park Barn Community Centre in June 2013. The destination blind has since been replaced by an electronic LED display. (*R. Kirwin*)

Adhering to the long tradition of having Setra coaches in the Farnham fleet, W295 UGX of that make stands outside the workshop building at Ewshot depot in April 2005. Although it was the last Setra purchased, it was similar W257 UGX/159 FCG that was the last out, in March 2012. (*R. Kirwin*)

As part of Safeguard's eightieth anniversary celebrations in April 2004, Les Ball drove vintage AEC Reliance 200 APB on the bus services, while his wife Betty returned specially to accompany him and to reprise her role as one of the last Safeguard conductresses. Note that the cat has been electronically-introduced into the photograph by a friend of Betty's but it would be a shame to take it out again! (*B. Ball Collection*)

SAFEGUARD COACHES

British & Continental Coach Hire Specialists

Celebrating 80 Years of Service

1924 - 2004

Day Excursions & Short Breaks

Tel: 01483 561103
www.safeguardcoaches.co.uk

started in May 2005 with Setra W257 UGX and finally completed in 2008, as part of the continuing integration of the Guildford and Farnham fleets. The Globus work finally finished at the end of the 2005 season, having become particularly unprofitable. No Day Excursions were run from Farnham from that year, while the Guildford programme was reduced.

Jane Newman and also Therese Hunter of Vancouver, Canada, daughter of Ken and Gill Newman, became directors from 1 May 2006. Mark Newman assumed a Non-Executive role following a move to Wales to pursue other career objectives and Andrew Halliday assumed the role of Managing Director.

Safeguard certainly had its fair share of employees who put in extremely long service for the company. 2007 marked the retirement of Alan Vineer, aged seventy-eight, who clocked up an amazing forty-six years of employment. Living in Westborough and Park Barn all his life, he started driving the buses in July 1961, later transferring to coach work. He subsequently worked at Ridgemount, opening the premises at 4.30 a.m., washing and fuelling vehicles and supervising the run-out. Being an organisation that recognises and rewards dedicated service, the management organised a farewell presentation and buffet lunch on his last day.

The cover of the 2004 excursions and tours brochure suitably reflected the eightieth anniversary and featured the 1931 Dennis GL coach.

Above left: Reflecting the two Volvo B10M/Plaxton Paragon coaches previously owned by Wallace Arnold of Leeds is Y758 HWT, purchased in September 2004 and now registered 531 FCG. Seen at Tonbridge School in September 2005. (*R. Kirwin*)

Above right: Safeguard's first Volvo B12M was YN05 HUY, new in March 2005. Delivered with fifty-three seats, it now has fifty-seven in its Plaxton Paragon body. This was the first new coach for general use (opposed to examples for Globus work and a seventy-seater for school duties) since 1998. (*R. Kirwin*)

Right: One of a pair of Volvo B12M/Plaxton Paragon acquired in December 2005 was YN04 WTL, now 247 FCG. (*K. Wheal Collection*)

Above: When a new bus was required in 2006, Safeguard stayed with the choice of Optare, but sampled a Tempo model. YJ06 FXM is in Epsom Road, Guildford, while assisting on Park & Ride service 300 from Merrow. (*R. Kirwin*)

Right: Alan Vineer retired in 2007 after a notable forty-six years of working for Safeguard. The celebratory send-off in the yard at Ridgemount was against an interesting backdrop of vehicles. Standing left to right are: Mark Smith, Andrew Halliday, Dave Gould (from Eagle Radio), Terry Cresswell, Heidi Millar, Marilyn Cresswell, Derek Holland, Linda Chambers. Peter Birch, Gordon Lambley (obscured), George Childs, Allan Ford, John Lake, Yvonne Lake, Michael Jennings, Reg Coulsdon, Bryan Karn, Pat Faull and Jane Newman. Seated from the left are Kit Newman, Alan Vineer and Toni Vineer. (*Safeguard Collection*)

A NOSTALGIC INTERLUDE

Looking back briefly to 'the old days', Alan Vineer recalls helping to dig by hand the inspection pit inside the garage and accidentally colliding with the front canopy of the Plaza cinema in Guildford, with a bus that was only two days old. In times gone by, the garage at Ridgemount was a place of inappropriate behaviour and harmless practical joking, much of which would be frowned on today, with its Health & Safety-conscious climate. At lunch time, some of the staff would take a nap in the boot of a coach; on one occasion it was then driven around the block by Mick Venables, giving the occupant(s) a rough ride. Graham Newman (known to the staff as 'Queenie'), Alan and some of the others would sit on a fine day in the yard, appreciating attractive young ladies going by. Even up to about ten years ago, Alan and Andrew Halliday would take large quantities of cash by van to the bank in the town centre, every day at 11 a.m., to the same place and by the same route, without giving any thought to possible consequences. The young Mark Newman was subjected to various pranks, such as putting a broom handle through his overalls while he was wearing them and putting him in a tall rubbish bin, while John Elliott stripped Mark to his underwear and then tied him for some time to a wheelbarrow. One day, Dave Cooke's steel toecaps were welded together with a MIG welder, while Dave was working under a car. Even Bern Newman got the treatment, when the rear of his Renault was jacked up for fun, with interesting consequences.

The garage was, nevertheless, a place of hard work, but a happy one that often resounded with laughter. Over the years, there were also a number of mishaps, ranging from vehicles accidentally being driven into the inspection pit (including a green company van that went by the name of 'Kermit', after the Muppet frog), to one ending up hanging over the wall at the rear of the Tubbs' hardware shop, after the handbrake was not properly applied. The bus stopped right against the back window of the shop and Joan Tubbs, who was inside at the time, wondered why it had suddenly gone dark. The Tubbs also suffered while excavations were occurring for an extension to the Safeguard garage – the garden retaining wall at their house in Ridgemount accidentally slipped downwards out of view.

Above left: Bert Newman, as some will still remember him. (*Newman Family Collection*)

Above right: The wedding of Ken and Gill Newman in 1949, Stoke Church, Guildford. Left to right are Bert, Ethel, Bernard, Ken and Gill Newman, Shirley (Gill's eldest sister), her husband Brian and Kit Newman. (*Newman Family Collection*)

Being a male domain, garage housekeeping was not a priority. The toilet was cleaned rarely and the sink in the old mess room in the workshop area was piled high with a mountain of discarded teabags, such that the water found it hard to drain away. The mugs were characterised by an oily coating of black grease on the outside and by a thick layer of tannin on the inside, being only rinsed out periodically.

Another long-serving driver was Brian Williams who transferred from Aldershot & District in 1963. His mother Rose was a conductress to driver Fred Page. Bill Clifton travelled home to lunch at Bellfields on Brian's bus and one day offered him a job at Safeguard. Brian thought he was joking as hardly ever were jobs with the company available. He recalls that the Westborough bus service was very busy with sometimes a thousand tickets issued during a shift. On market days, the buses would be required to carry back to Westborough all manner of goods from town, accompanying the purchaser, including live chickens and piglets, tin baths and planks of wood. One Christmas, a character called Monty Mortimer (allegedly arrested at some point for being drunk on a pushbike) stood at the front of the bus for several trips and orchestrated community carol singing, while collecting money for the driver and conductor. When he had finished, Brian got more than a week's wages in tips. Another time, a passenger would travel around dressed as Father Christmas. Sunday mornings in summer would be spent with a coach parked in North Street, near Guildford Library, with chalk-written boards alongside, advertising that afternoon's or evening's Mystery Drive. Aldershot & District would do the same, but Safeguard usually got more bookings. Those signing-up for a Mystery Drive would usually be male,

with crates of bottled beer being loaded into the boot of the coach for consuming at stopping points. The only 'mystery' relating to the itinerary, was which pub(s) the coach would be stopping at this time, but the scenery mattered little. Later, Brian was most upset when the Park Barn service was extended from the Youth Centre to the shopping parade. The drivers had what they called 'tea houses' near the old terminus, where a free cuppa was often waiting; by extending the route, these locations were now geographically inappropriate.

Right: Label displayed in coaches hired by Safeguard from other operators.

ON HIRE TO
SAFEGUARD
COACHES LTD.

MODERN SAFEGUARD – RECENT DEVELOPMENTS

Fast-forwarding again into the present century, in Surrey, Senior Citizens had for a considerable time enjoyed a Concessionary Fare scheme whereby half-rate travel was permitted after 9 a.m., Mondays to Fridays and any time at weekends. When the government enacted legislation for a free travel scheme for the Over 60s, from April 2006, the number of pensioners riding on Safeguard buses rose by 30 to 35 per cent within a couple of months, with an overall increase in ridership of 5 to 6 per cent. In April 2008, the free travel scheme became England-wide. With administration of it moving from Borough and District Councils to the upper tier authority, such as Surrey County Council, from April 2011, the government issued new guidelines for local authorities in terms of the formula to be used for calculating re-imbursement to bus companies for revenue forgone. The lower payments received, produced a budgetary pressure for some operators, especially those carrying large numbers of Over 60s.

In the 1960s, Graham Chivers started his coach business at Elstead, undertaking private hire and school contracts. A good relationship was always maintained with Safeguard and towards the end of 2006 Graham approached them regarding a possible sale as he was seeking to scale down his operations. Thus, in February 2007, Safeguard acquired the Chivers goodwill, name, telephone number and advance order book, together with a Mercedes Benz 1223L/Optare Solera coach. Andrew Norris, Graham Chivers' son in law also transferred as a driver. However, Chivers continued for some time to run a Mercedes Benz Vario midi coach on a school contract, this being driven by his daughter Suzanne.

In December 2006, a new thirty-six-seat Mercedes Tourino coach was acquired, the first coach in the fleet fitted with a Euro 4 – rated engine, to satisfy the forthcoming London Low Emission Zone requirements. However, subsequent additions to the coach fleet at both Guildford and Farnham have been standardised on Volvos, both new and from previous owners, with either Plaxton or Van Hool bodywork. The bus fleet for the town services saw the arrival between October 2008 and January 2011 of three Optare Versas – MX58 ABF, YJ10 EZT and YJ60 LRO. These have Cummins engines, as opposed to Mercedes in the Excels and Tempo. Having latterly been stored after use as a reserve for the Guildford Shuttle service, the last step-entrance bus was disposed of in August 2011, being

When a smaller coach was required in 2006, a Mercedes Benz Tourino with thirty-six seats was chosen. BX56 VTM offered the attractive appearance and many of the features of larger vehicles. Daily hand-washing results in the normal immaculate appearance of Safeguard's vehicles. Seen at The Royal Grammar School's Chilworth playing fields. (*Safeguard Collection*)

The third of three Volvo B12B/Van Hool Alicron coaches bought new in 2007/8 was WA58 EOO, seen posed at the west front of Guildford Cathedral in September 2011– a popular local location for Safeguard photo-shoots. The driver is Nigel Cotton. (*Safeguard Collection*)

sold for preservation on the Isle of Wight. This was H577 MOC, a Dennis Dart with Carlyle bodywork, which before acquisition in January 2000 had been rebuilt by the Fleetmaster dealership with a Plaxton Pointer front.

Virtually all Day Excursions from the Guildford area were cancelled in 2006, if any further proof was needed of the significant decline in this sector of the market, and none at all were run from the 2007 season, as they were no longer worthwhile to the company. This was the end of a very long tradition stretching right back to Safeguard's founding in 1924. Senior Citizens had latterly been the main customers and perhaps now that free bus travel was available to them, they were making more trips by that mode of transport.

Having once been a driving force in the business, but latterly unable to directly participate through illness, Bern Newman died in June 2009, aged eighty-three, while his wife Kit ceased to be a Director in March 2008; she passed away in January 2011.

Both Bernard and Ken Newman commanded great respect from the staff as they treated them as one of the family, on first name terms. Bern was always polite, even when very displeased by something that had been done, such as when a coach collided with the yard gate post for the second time with the same driver, after Bern had just finished repairing it after the first encounter. If he spotted any bodywork damage, he would never let a coach leave the yard until he had repaired it as good as new, taking all night if necessary. If he saw dirty coach windows, he would comment to the driver 'you have a nice set of curtains', which really meant clean them immediately. Shortly after Farnham Coaches had been acquired in 1988, he noted one of the Setra coaches in the yard at Guildford and was heard to say 'get it out – I'm not having any foreign motors here!'

The company sought and was granted in April 2008, a three year validity residential planning permission to allow the re-development of the Ridgemount site, which is really of insufficient size for current operations. There were also efforts made to see if the Guildford and Farnham operations could be combined on one site, although rising fuel costs would have been exacerbated by more 'dead mileage'. However, plans to relocate one or both depots to an alternative site were thwarted by an inability to find a suitable location, against a background of national economic downturn and that on balance, the smartest potential could be gained from retaining two bases. The planning permission for the construction of thirteen flats was subsequently renewed to expire in July 2016 – just in case.

The Guildford Shuttle service was originally offered on an annual contract basis, which Safeguard managed to secure each time it was tendered. Eventually a three year contract was obtained, but in due course, the Borough Council decided that it no longer wished to fund it. It was withdrawn after 30 August 2008, despite strong protests from users and other people in the community. A partial replacement in the form of a demand-responsive pre-bookable service was offered, run with one of the Guildford Dial-A-Ride minibuses. However, this was viewed as an inadequate alternative and saw negligible support. The intense campaign for re-instatement continued, with much media interest and as a service to the local community, Safeguard re-introduced it on 12 January 2009 as a commercial venture, charging a £1 flat fare to those not entitled to free travel with a Concessionary Fare permit. The occasion was attended by local MP, Anne Milton, and by Hon. Freeman Bill Bellerby, who had led the campaign and who was delighted to discover that Dennis Dart VU02 TTJ now carried his name. However, the service made a loss and drivers did not relish the prospect of going round and round the town all day on a route with a difficult corner which resulted in periodic vehicle damage. Therefore, its last day was 22 May 2010, which coincided with some major changes to the other town services the next day. Despite

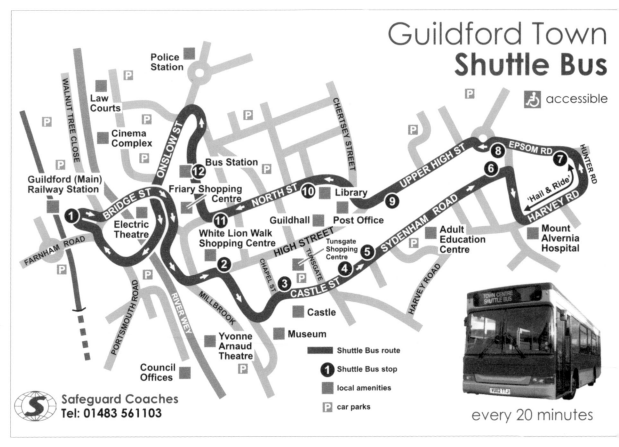

Guildford Town Shuttle Bus

♿ accessible

Police Station

Law Courts

Cinema Complex

WALNUT TREE CLOSE

ONSLOW ST

Guildford (Main) Railway Station

BRIDGE ST

FARNHAM ROAD

Electric Theatre

Friary Shopping Centre

12

Bus Station

White Lion Walk Shopping Centre

11

NORTH ST

10

Library

Guildhall

Post Office

CHERTSEY STREET

UPPER HIGH ST

8 EPSOM RD 7

6

'Hail & Ride'

HUNTER RD

HARVEY RD

Mount Alvernia Hospital

9

SYDENHAM ROAD

Adult Education Centre

HIGH STREET

Tunsgate Shopping Centre

TUNSGATE

5

4

HARVEY ROAD

2

CHAPEL ST

3

CASTLE ST

PORTSMOUTH ROAD

RIVER WEY

MILLBROOK

Castle

Museum

Yvonne Arnaud Theatre

Council Offices

▬▬ Shuttle Bus route

① Shuttle Bus stop

■ local amenities

🅿 car parks

Safeguard Coaches
Tel: 01483 561103

every 20 minutes

Above left: The new coaches for 2009 were two Volvo B12Ms with Plaxton Panther bodywork, registered YN58 NCC/NDD. The first in the fleet of 12.8 m length, they generally operate from the Ewshot yard due to space constraints at Guildford; this one has Peter Pearson at the wheel. (*K. Wheal Collection*)

Above right: The route of the Guildford Town Shuttle on re-introduction on a commercial basis in 2009.

another vociferous campaign, the Borough Council was not moved to offer a subsidy.

The long-standing student nurse transport contract for the University of Surrey was terminated due to funding cuts in December 2009, eight months earlier than a planned re-tendering. This caused a loss of turnover for Safeguard of £250,000 per year, although as the coaches were needed for other work, there was little opportunity to reduce costs accordingly. However, some new school work helped make up for the loss. Overall, though, Safeguard has grown its business, such that turnover rose 12 per cent between 2002 and 2010 and the average profit made between 2007 and 2011 was double that achieved in 2003 to 2006. Profitability was aided by changes of working practices and better integration between the Guildford and Farnham based fleets, hence the harmonising of coach liveries. All maintenance work at both sites was put under the control of engineering manager Brett Lambley in 2007. In 2011 there were fourteen coaches at Farnham, thirteen at Guildford and eleven operational buses at Guildford, as well as the AEC Reliance 200 APB.

The current remits of the Office of Fair Trading and the Competition Commission, while potentially helpful to the general consumer, are somewhat unwelcome in the bus industry, where the catch-all Competition Act propagates constraints that prevent common-sense integration of services, fare structures and ticket products. Achieving service co-ordination between competing operators in the interests of the travelling public are deals that dare not be made, for fear of breaking competition law. However, the enactment of the Transport Act 2008 included provisions for local authorities to act as 'honest brokers' and to endorse proposed co-ordination schemes as being helpful in the wider sense. One such Qualifying Agreement, proposed by Safeguard and brokered by Surrey County Council, allowed Arriva and Safeguard to make beneficial improvements to services 3, 4 and 5, by ending the constraints of long-standing joint operation.

The Agreement gave an opportunity for better provision and control of the Park Barn routes, without the fear of a competitive skirmish with Arriva on a tit-for-tat basis. From 23 May 2010, Safeguard surrendered its share of service 3 to Bellfields, leaving Arriva in sole charge. In reciprocation, Arriva withdrew its workings on service 4 in favour of Safeguard and the revenue support from the County Council for evening journeys also transferred. Daytime frequency was increased to every fifteen minutes on each of services 3, 4 and 5, meaning that between Guildford and Park Barn there was, for once, a move in the positive direction with eight journeys per hour instead of six.

Apart from the freedom to increase frequencies, without upsetting the other operator, the benefits of the Agreement included an ability for improved scheduling to aid operational reliability, more effective regulation and control including through the data provided by the Real Time Information system, better perception of the product by the public through clearer 'service ownership' and the best possible chance for ongoing growth and viability without impacting adversely on the overall competitive balance between Safeguard and Arriva in Guildford. Services 4 and 5 were re-launched as 'into town' with an attractive leaflet delivered to homes along the routes and with a dedicated website.

With partnership investment from Arriva and Safeguard, Surrey County Council had provided the Real Time Information system as early as 2003, although it was some time before it became fully-robust due to technical difficulties. The movement of buses is plotted by the system, allowing the actual minutes before the bus arrives to be displayed on electronic signs at certain stops and through a public-access website. There are also computer screens at Ridgemount which allow the position

Above left: A new Optare Versa (YJ10 EZT) arrived in May 2010, ready for Safeguard to become the sole provider of services 4 and 5 to Park Barn for the first time since 1992. (*Optare Group*)

Above right: Two of the three Dennis Dart/East Lancs Myllennium vehicles owned by Surrey County Council and used by Safeguard from July 2010 until August 2013, pass in Epsom Road on service 300 to and from the Merrow Park & Ride site, in May 2013. (*R. Kirwin*)

Right: Another Optare Versa, YJ60 LRO, arrived in January 2011. (*R. Kirwin*)

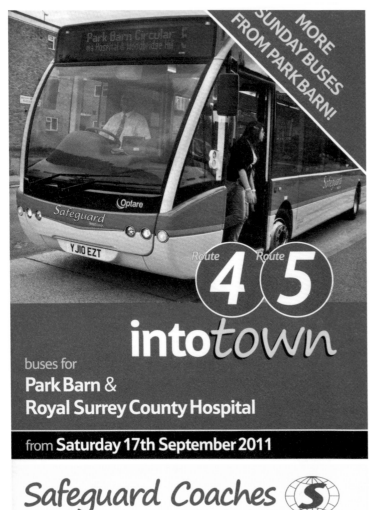

of each bus to be seen on a map display. Service controllers can regulate the buses by radio to the drivers, if they are widely at variance with the timetable. There is also an 'intelligent traffic signal' function, whereby a transponder on an approaching bus can turn the traffic lights to green earlier than would have been the case, if the bus is running late.

In February 2010, Safeguard installed a vehicle and driver monitoring system supplied by Green Road Technologies, which analyses driving style attributes and reports them to the driver and to the management. Since introduction, there has been a marked reduction in the frequency of accidents, reduced fuel use and reduced wear and tear on vehicles. The supplier has recently changed to Traffilog, which also allows vehicle performance through fault codes to be monitored and the driver's use of the operating pedals to be tracked, so that poor driving habits can be identified and corrected. Safeguard is the first local coach operator to install these telematics.

Between January 2006 and July 2010, Surrey County Council ran its 'Pegasus' school transport scheme to various primary schools, as a way of discouraging parents of children not entitled to free transport, from using their cars. The services carried an Escort, to further enhance the safety and security of students aged five to eleven. A dedicated fleet of twenty-two low-floor, long Dennis Darts with East Lancs Myllennium bodywork was purchased by the Council and operated under contract by First Beeline Buses Ltd from Council premises at Merrow, just outside Guildford. A limited amount of off-peak private hire and local bus service work was also carried out with Pegasus vehicles, including a new Park and Ride service numbered 300 on weekdays into Guildford town centre from a purpose-built site run by Guildford Borough Council on the Epsom Road A25 just east of Merrow.

With the cessation of Pegasus approaching, the Council issued a tender for continuation of service 300, with the option of using three of the Pegasus fleet, to be staffed, maintained and insured by the successful bidder. Fortunately for Safeguard, which had recently lost the University work, the contract was won and was effective from 24 July 2010. Three of the Dennis Darts were leased to Safeguard for a peppercorn amount (LK06 BWB, LK07 CBO/CBU) and were put into a special Park and Ride livery inspired by Safeguard's traditional red colour scheme. Two drivers transferred under employment protection rules from First Beeline and spent their time solely on service 300. The route was via Epsom Road, but on Mondays to Fridays, a diversion was made via Boxgrove Road and London Road, so as to stop near a Surrey County Council office in Cross Lanes for the benefit of staff. However, from 17 September 2011 all journeys operated straight along the Epsom Road, following the closure of the Council's office.

Over the years, Safeguard had run a number of Surrey County Council local public bus services provided primarily for specific schools. One, numbered 823, was taken on short-term in March 2011 from Grange Park and Bellfields to George Abbot School, after the Council had terminated a contract with Countryliner. This ceased four months later along with the other remaining example of such a service – the 815 from West Clandon, Ripley and Send to the same school. Since September 2011, home to school transport work has been purely for private schools, including Tormead in Guildford, St. Catherine's at Bramley, Priorsfield at Godalming, Frensham Heights (near Farnham), Salesian College at Farnborough, Alton Convent and St Nicholas at Church Crookham. In addition, ten schools were using Safeguard and Farnham Coaches for the transport of students to swimming lessons and to sports fixtures.

At the Operator Excellence Awards in October 2011, sponsored by 'Route One' magazine, Andrew Halliday was named Coach Manager of the Year, while Safeguard was shortlisted for Small Bus Operator of the

Above left: Andrew Halliday receives the accolade of Coach Manager of the Year at the 'Route One' Operator Excellence Awards in October 2011. (*Route One magazine*)

Above right: SN09 JUX is one of three Volvo B10B/Van Hool Alizee coaches previously owned by AAA of Kirknewton, which were purchased in November 2011. They entered service in March 2012 and are based at Ewshot. The location is the RNLI College at Poole, Dorset. (*Safeguard Collection*)

Right: The most recent coach to be purchased is seventy-seat Volvo B7R/Plaxton Profile SN60 FMO, also for the Farnham Coaches fleet. Seen in the grounds of Charterhouse School in July 2012. (*R. Kirwin*)

Year. Previously, in 2006, Brett Lambley had won Bus Engineer of the Year at the equivalent Awards.

Despite the difficult economic climate and the loss of some traditional private hire business due to the London Olympics, poor weather and the Queen's Diamond Jubilee, 2012 was a good year for Safeguard and Farnham Coaches with a turnover approaching £3.3 million. Approximately 34 per cent of this came from bus services, 46 per cent from private hire and 20 per cent from contract work. Three coaches were provided for three weeks round-the-clock on sub-contract to another operator to provide the transport for Metropolitan Police officers to various Olympic venues; coaches were also provided for the Nigerian Basketball Team and the British Synchronised Swimming Team. Contracted shopping trips into Guildford for the staff of British Oxygen Company at Surrey Research Park, were won from Countryliner, following its demise. On the Park Barn bus services, 731,000 passenger journeys were made in the year ending March 2012 (7 per cent up on 2011 and 15 per cent up on 2009/10), increasing to 738,000 in the year ending March 2013, in contrast to the national trend outside London. This was despite the challenge of a national financial recession. To support Andrew Halliday, Matthew Tighe was appointed Operations Manager in December 2012, supported by Heidi Millar and Maureen Guyan. The last Setra coach (W257 UGX) and the Mercedes/Hispano (W417 HOB) were sold in March 2012, resulting in 80 per cent of the coach fleet being on Volvo chassis. Three pre-owned Volvo B12B/Van Hool coaches went into use that March, having been purchased four months earlier, to be followed by a 2010 Volvo B7R/Plaxton (SN60 FMO) in April, part-exchanged for the Setra and the Mercedes.

Safeguard's service 4/5 fares were last revised in October 2012 and are only reviewed when absolutely necessary, rather than routinely. Adult single fares range from £1.00 to £1.80 and return fares from £1.60 to £2.90. They also offer Day tickets and Weekly and Monthly Season Tickets. Before 9.30 a.m., Concessionary Fare Permit holders may travel for £1.20. A new period ticket purchase option, known as M-ticket, is available by using a mobile phone, facilitated by Mobile OnBoard.

Gill Newman passed away on 18 June 2013, aged eighty-three, at her home in Oxfordshire, where she had lived since her husband Ken died in 2001. She retained a keen interest in the company to the end, being the last representative of the third generation of Newmans. She was much looking forward to the company's ninetieth anniversary and has contributed some memories to this book. A couple of weeks later, there occurred the death of Derek ('Dutch') Holland, who worked for Safeguard from 1995 until 2010 as a coach driver, foreman and latterly Assistant Operations Manager. July 2013 marked the retirement of bus driver Emilio Dubra, who came to Britain in 1966 from Spain. After four years of farming in Byfleet, he became a conductor for Aldershot & District and then a driver/conductor for Alder Valley. In 1986 he transferred to Safeguard and clocked up a noteworthy twenty-seven-and-a-half years of service, which for much of that time included working every Sunday that he legally could.

In spring 2013, Surrey County Council invited new tenders for the Park and Ride services in Guildford, operated by Arriva and Safeguard. The contracts for all the services were awarded to Stagecoach on price and therefore Safeguard's last day on service 300 was 31 August. Safeguard's operational performance had been excellent but the Council had to make a business decision, which in no way reflected any dissatisfaction with Safeguard's service delivery or presentation. The three Dennis Darts leased by Safeguard from the County Council passed to Stagecoach as part of the new contract arrangements.

As this story draws to a close, it can be noted that in autumn 2013, the Safeguard fleet was formed of nine buses, twenty-six coaches and the heritage AEC Reliance bus. Bus service mileage for the year ending

Above left: A new modular office Portakabin is put into place at the Farnham Coaches yard in Ewshot, replacing one twenty-five years old and originally intended to last for ten. In 2013, the company's finance office activities moved to Ewshot from the now somewhat cramped premises at Ridgemount Garage. (*Safeguard Collection*)

Above right: The latest Optare Versa bus, runs up Farnham Road in October 2013 on its first revenue earning job – a school contract for the Guildford County School, driven by Roy Cooke. YD63 UZJ is regarded as a 'dual purpose' model – suitable for both bus service and coaching duties. It has thirty-seven high-backed seats, three point seat-belts and a tachograph. (*R. Kirwin*)

May 2014 is expected to be 217,000, excluding service 300. The company employs forty-eight full time people – thirteen bus drivers, twenty coach drivers, four engineers and nine management and administration staff. In addition there is sixteen part-time staff, of which fourteen are drivers.

Meanwhile, innovation continues as the bus fleet is to become the first in Guildford to be fitted with free wi-fi for passengers, with part-funding from Surrey County Council using Local Sustainable Transport Funding money, under the Travel Smart initiative.

FINAL REFLECTIONS

Having now examined the varying fortunes of the business over the years, it is perhaps appropriate for some concluding thoughts on why Safeguard has survived for ninety years, to come from the firm itself. The bus and coach industry is interesting and challenging, not least because it is people dependent, relying on the support of staff, suppliers and customers. Through all the whimsical changes of government transport policy, Safeguard has had to adapt. The ability to plan long term for consolidation or growth as required, rather than over-reacting to short term opportunities or challenges, has been a major strength, while the Newman family has recognised the need to use outside expertise where prudent to do so. Safeguard is a survivor, based on attention to detail and adaptability. It is confident of what it is but not churlish enough to think that it can rest on its laurels. Further change will no doubt need to follow if its past success is carried forward by future generations.

The very last words come from Andrew Halliday:

It is of course the people who are the lifeblood and bedrock of the industry and in many cases they are the 'salt of the earth' and real 'characters'. In my experience they are generally great people to work with, down to earth, honest and hard-working. Safeguard has had a vast variety of employees – some quite exceptional and surprising – including former policemen, hoteliers and head teachers. I believe that drivers and engineers especially have thankless tasks and deserve more respect than they get from managers, the travelling public and society as a whole. A few 'bad apples' are very much in the minority. I reject the notion that it's 'not like the old days' and to imply that the job was better and more enjoyable then, is to look through rose-tinted spectacles and to denigrate the current workforce. I would recommend working in this industry, but you will rarely get rich quick, you'll have to work hard, sometimes at crazy hours in unglamorous circumstances and at times you'll get very misunderstood! Safeguard has been part of the fabric of Guildford in the past, the present and (we believe) will be in the future.

Above: Three Farnham Coaches vehicles stand in the Bottom Yard at Ewshot depot. (*Safeguard Collection*)

Left: Sold by Safeguard in May 1988, Leyland Leopard OPC 26R passed through a number of owners but happily is now owned by Richard Kirwin, who has restored it to original condition. He purchased it from Emblings Coaches in Cambridgeshire in March 2005. Where better to pose it but Cabell Road in Park Barn? (*R. Kirwin*)

APPENDIX 1

Safeguard Bus Services October 1986 To Present

G3

At 26.10.86: Guildford–Stoke–Bellfields Estate (Hazel Avenue) (Mondays to Saturdays). Operated jointly with Alder Valley, later Alder Valley West Surrey, later Guildford & West Surrey Buses, later Arriva.

25.7.98: 'G' route number prefix removed.

4.9.99: Evening journeys taken over from Arriva.

24.7.03: Evening journeys withdrawn.

23.5.10: Withdrawn by Safeguard and operated wholly by Arriva.

G4

At 26.10.86: Guildford–Woodbridge–Southway–Chapelhouse–Park Barn–Southway–Woodbridge–Guildford (Daily). Some off-peak journeys Monday–Friday divert via Park Barn Drive and Barnwood Road.

31.8.88: Diverted on Sundays from Southway to/from Royal Surrey County Hospital.

29.4.91: Revised on Mondays to Saturdays to return to Guildford from Park Barn via Royal Surrey County Hospital and Guildford Park. Some journeys also serve Surrey Research Park. Journeys via Barnwood Road diverted via standard route along Cabell Road.

15.8.94: Revised on Mondays to Saturdays to operate both ways via Woodbridge and Southway. Barnwood Road diversion reintroduced on Mondays to Saturdays.

28.1.95: Part of daytime service on Mondays to Saturdays transferred to Guildford & West Surrey Buses, later Arriva.

25.3.97: Some Monday–Friday midday journeys diverted into Guildford Business Park.

26.7.97: On Mondays to Saturdays reverted to circular working, outward via Woodbridge, return via Guildford Park. Business Park diversion ceased.

25.7.98: 'G' route number prefix removed.

26.7.03: Journeys via Barnwood Road diverted via standard route along Cabell Road.

10.1.04: Evening journeys (Daily) taken over by Arriva.

23.5.10 All Arriva journeys transferred back to Safeguard.

G5

At 26.10.86: Guildford–Guildford Park–Royal Surrey County Hospital–Chapelhouse–Park Barn–Royal Surrey County Hospital–Guildford Park–Guildford (Daily). Some off-peak journeys Monday–Friday divert via Park Barn Drive and Barnwood Road.

15.6.87: Some journeys diverted Mondays to Saturdays into Post House Hotel or Surrey Research Park.

31.1.88: Withdrawn on Sundays. Post House Hotel diversion withdrawn.

29.4.91: Revised to return to Guildford from Park Barn via Southway and Woodbridge. Journeys via Barnwood Road diverted via standard route along Cabell Road.

15.8.94: Revised to operate both ways via Guildford Park and Hospital. Barnwood Road diversion re-introduced on Mondays to Saturdays.

26.7.97: Reverted to circular working, outward via Guildford Park, return via Woodbridge.

25.7.98: 'G' route number prefix removed.

26.7.03: Journeys via Barnwood Road diverted via standard route along Cabell Road.

546

26.10.86: Cock Hill–Elstead–Royal Common–Shackleford–Hurtmore–Charterhouse–Godalming (Monday to Saturday peak hours, also operated off-peak Tuesday, Wednesday, Friday and Saturday Shackleford–Godalming) Previously part of Alder Valley 246.

11.86: Additional afternoon schoolday journey: Godalming to Cock Hill, returning via Elstead and Milford to Godalming.

12.5.87: Off-peak journeys extended from Godalming to Farncombe Meadrow–Peasmarsh–Guildford.

24.10.87: Withdrawn.

550

26.10.86: Camberley–Ravenswood–Portsmouth Road–Frimley Park Hospital–Frimley–Frimley Green–Mytchett–Ash Vale–Ash Wharf–Dover Arms–Ash–Ash Green–Tongham–Aldershot (Mondays to Saturdays). Some journeys via Park Road and Frimley Road between Camberley and Frimley and some journeys via Shawfields Road between Ash Wharf and Ash. Previously Alder Valley 450.

29.8.92: Withdrawn and taken over by Alder Valley.

559.659

26.10.86: Byfleet–Manor Farm–West Byfleet–Pyrford–Maybury Inn–Sheerwater (Bishop David Brown School) (Schooldays) Previously London Country 837.

24.7.92: Withdrawn and taken over by London & Country.

6.9.94: Re-instated as service 659, taken over from London & Country.

20.12.96: Withdrawn.

G10

5.5.87: New service: Guildford–Woodbridge–Westway–Foxburrows Avenue–Royal Surrey County Hospital–Guildford Park–Guildford (Mondays to Saturdays).

3.8.87: Revised to operate: Guildford–Woodbridge–Southway–Foxburrows Avenue–Westway–Woodbridge–Guildford.

4.7.88: Revised to operate: Guildford–Woodbridge–Northway–Westway–Foxburrows Avenue–Royal Surrey County Hospital–Guildford Park–Guildford (in this direction only).

10.1.91: Diverted after Northway via Rydes Hill and Worplesdon Road to return to Guildford via Woodbridge.

29.4.91: Revised to operate: Guildford–Guildford Park–Hospital–Roundhill Way–Westway–Northway–Canterbury Road–Broadacres–Clover Road–Foxburrows Avenue–Hospital–Guildford Park–Guildford.

6.1.92: Revised to operate: Guildford–Woodbridge–Westway–Foxburrows Avenue–Clover Road–Applegarth Avenue–Park Barn–Hospital–Guildford Park–Guildford.

1.9.92: Revised to operate: Guildford–Woodbridge–Broadacres–Applegarth Avenue–Park Barn–Pondmeadows–Foxburrows Avenue–Hospital–Guildford Park–Guildford (in this direction only).

5.4.93: Diverted between Broadacres and Foxburrows Avenue via Park Barn Drive.

15.8.94: Revised to operate: Guildford–Guildford Park–Tesco–Hospital–Foxburrows Avenue–Park Barn Drive–Barnwood Road–Applegarth Avenue–Park Barn–Hospital–Tesco–Guildford Park–Guildford (in this direction only).

17.9.94: Withdrawn.

G11

5.5.87: New service: Guildford–Woodbridge–Westway, then via Fairlands Estate or via Broadacres and Wood Street Green to Clasford Bridge–Normandy–Ash (Mondays to Saturdays).

3.8.87: Revised to operate direct from Woodbridge to Fairlands Estate.

10.1.91: Withdrawn.

20.9.93: New service: Guildford–Guildford Park–Hospital–Park Barn–Broadacres–Wood Street–Woodbridge–Guildford (Tuesdays, Thursdays and Saturdays).

15.8.94: Withdrawn and number re–used for new service: Guildford–Cross Lanes–Tormead Road–Boxgrove Lane–Merrow Woods–Bushy Hill (Mondays to Saturdays).

17.10.94: Withdrawn on Saturdays, peak hour journeys diverted direct via London Road to Boxgrove Lane and extended in Bushy Hill to include Sheeplands Avenue.

28.1.95: Revised to operate: Research Park (Monday–Friday peak hours and midday)–Hospital–Tesco–Guildford Park–Guildford–Cross Lanes–Tormead Road–Boxgrove Lane–Merrow Woods–Bushy Hill (Mondays to Saturdays).

31.7.95: Withdrawn between Research Park and Guildford, diverted via Boxgrove Park and curtailed to terminate at Merrow (Great Goodwins Drive).

26.7.97: Extended again from Guildford to Hospital.Research Park.

25.7.98: 'G' route number prefix removed. Except for one Monday–Friday morning peak journey from the Hospital, curtailed to operate Guildford to Great Goodwins Drive.

30.11.98: One journey each way Mondays to Fridays extended to start. finish at Guildford Park, rather than Hospital.

27.1.01: Guildford Park journeys reduced to schooldays only.

31.8.02: Withdrawn and taken over by Countryliner.

G9

3.8.87: New service: Guildford–Woodbridge–Northway–Worplesdon Road–Grange Park (Mondays to Saturdays). During Monday–Friday peak hours, operated direct via Worplesdon Road rather than Northway. Replaced Alder Valley 9 and 15.

4.7.88: revised to be the reverse of G10 (qv).

10.1.91: Withdrawn.

29.4.91: New service: Guildford–Woodbridge–Westway–Foxburrows Avenue–Clover Road–Broadacres–Lincoln Road–Northway–Woodbridge–Guildford (Mondays to Saturdays).

6.1.92: Revised to operate between Guildford and Broadacres via Guildford Park–Hospital–Park Barn and Applegarth Avenue.

1.9.92: Revised to be the reverse of G10 (qv).

5.4.93: Revised to operate: Guildford–Guildford Park–Hospital–Park Barn–Applegarth Avenue–Broadacres–Wood Street–Guildford.

15.8.94: Revised to be the reverse of G10 (qv).

17.10.94: Revised to operate: Guildford–Guildford Park–Tesco–Hospital (Mondays to Fridays), extended to Research Park during peak hours.

28.1.95: Withdrawn.

31.7.95: Re–introduced from Guildford to Hospital (Mondays to Saturdays), extended to Research Park during peak hours and midday, Mondays to Fridays.

26.7.97: Withdrawn.

542

3.9.87: New service: Ewhurst–Ewhurst Green–Ellens Green–Cox Green–Baynards–Alfold Crossways–Dunsfold–Loxhill–Hascombe–Winkworth–Busbridge–Godalming College (Schooldays).

20.7.90: Withdrawn and taken over by Tillingbourne Bus Co.

G12

20.9.93: New service: Guildford–Woodbridge–Wood Street–Broadacres–Park Barn Drive–Foxburrows Avenue–Hospital–Guildford Park–Guildford (Tuesdays, Thursdays and Saturdays).

15.8.94: Withdrawn and number re–used for new service: Guildford–London Road–Boxgrove Lane–Merrow Woods–Bushy Hill (Mondays to Saturdays).

17.10.94: Revised to operate: Guildford–Epsom Road–Bushy Hill (Mondays to Fridays).

28.1.95: Withdrawn.

514

4.10.93: New service: Shortheath–Burnt Hill Road–Lodge Hill Road–Abbot's Ride–Farnham–Sainsburys–Hale–North Avenue–Heath End–Upper Weybourne Lane–Knights Road (Mondays to Fridays).

27.5.94: Withdrawn and taken over by Frimley Coaches.

686

6.9.94: New service: Westfield–Mayford–Sutton Green–Grangefield Estate–Jacobs Well–Burpham–George Abbot School (Schooldays).

23.7.02: Withdrawn and taken over by Countryliner.

16

6.1.97: New service: Dockenfield–Bucks Horn Oak–Holt Pound Bottom–Rowledge–Boundstone–Shortheath–Ridgway Road–Menin Way–Farnham–Sainsburys (Mondays to Saturdays), with schoolday and Monday to Friday morning peak journeys extended to Badshot Lea, Boxalls Lane and Aldershot. Replaced Stagecoach Hants & Surrey.

3.5.97: Withdrawn and taken over by Tillingbourne.

690

3.2.97: Pirbright–Pirbright Camp–Brookwood–Winston Churchill School–St Johns–Wych Hill–Kingfield Green (Schooldays) Previously operated by Hills of Hersham.

2.9.97: Morning journey extended to start at Fox Corner.

7.9.99: Afternoon journey extended to Fox Corner.

27.9.99: Diverted between Fox Corner and Pirbright via Stanford Common.

14.4.00: Withdrawn and taken over by White Rose.

103

22.11.97: Short term Park and Ride service: University of Surrey–Guildford town centre (Saturdays until 14.2.98).

102

29.11.97: Short term Park and Ride service: George Abbot School–Guildford town centre (Saturdays until 27.12.97).

10

25.7.98: New service: Guildford–Charlotteville–Warren Road–Boxgrove Park (Mondays to Saturdays) to replace Arriva 1 and 18.

30.11.98: Diverted to operate via Epsom Road instead of York Road.

27.1.01: Extended from Boxgrove Park to Merrow Woods and Great Goodwins Drive.

31.8.02: Withdrawn and taken over by Countryliner.

14

25.7.98: New service: Guildford–Woodbridge–Northway–Rydes Hill–Westway–Woodside Road–Foxburrows Avenue–Hospital–Guildford Park–Guildford (Mondays to Saturdays). To replace Arriva 14.

28.11.98: Withdrawn.

699

7.9.99: Pirbright–Stanford Common–Fox Corner–Worplesdon–Fairlands–Wood Street–George Abbot School (Schooldays) Previously operated by Edward Thomas & Son.

23.7.02: Withdrawn and taken over by Fleetwing Travel.

Town Shuttle

4.9.00: New service: Guildford Bus Station–Rail Station–Lower High Street–Sydenham Road–Upper High Street–North Street–Bus Station (Mondays to Saturdays).

18.12.00: Revised to commence and terminate at Rail Station.

30.8.08: Withdrawn.

12.1.09: Re–introduced and diverted via Harvey Road.

22.5.10: Withdrawn.

815

15.11.00: Fetcham–Bookham–Preston Cross–Effingham–Effingham Junction–Horsley Station–West Horsley–Ripley–Newark Lane–Send Marsh–Send–Burnt Common–George Abbot School–St. Peter's School (Schooldays). Previously operated by North Surrey Buses.

23.4.01: Withdrawn between Fetcham and Effingham Junction.

3.9.08: Revised to operate: Clandon Crossroads–West Clandon–Burnt Common–Ripley then as before.

20.4.09: Diverted between Send Marsh and Burnt Common via Send Marsh Road.

22.7.11: Withdrawn.

825

15.11.00: St. Bede's School–Burnt Common–Ripley–Newark Lane (Schoolday afternoons). Previously operated by North Surrey Buses.

18.2.11: Withdrawn.

29, 38, 534, 535, 546–549, 565, 688, 698

16.9.02: Replacing Stagecoach Hants & Surrey:

29 Farley Green–Little London–Albury Heath–Albury–Chilworth Station–Blackheath–Wonersh–Shalford–Guildford (Mondays and Thursdays).

38 Guildford–Worplesdon Road–Grange Park–Stoughton–Bellfields–Slyfield Green–Burpham Sainsburys (Tuesdays and Fridays).

534 Farnham–Tilford–Shortfield Common–Millbridge–Frensham–Rowledge–Burnt Hill Road–Lodge Hill Road–Farnham (Tuesdays, Wednesdays and Fridays).

535 Milford–Thursley–Pride of the Valley–Rushmoor–Tilford–Abbots Ride–Farnham–Marston Road (Mondays to Fridays).

546 Christmaspie–Wyke–Ash Station–Ash Green–Tongham–Runfold–Sainsburys–Farnham (Mondays and Thursdays).

547 Farnham–Runfold–The Sands–Seale–Puttenham–Christmaspie–Wyke–Dolleys Hill–Normandy–Fairlands–Hospital–Guildford (Tuesdays and Fridays).

548 Farnham–Badshot Lea–Ash–Tongham–Ash Green–Ash Station–Wyke–Christmaspie–Normandy–Fairlands–Worplesdon–Mayford–Woking (Wednesdays).

549 Farnham–Runfold–Tongham–Ash Green–Ash Station–Wyke–Christmaspie–Wanborough–Sunnydown–Guildford (Mondays and Thursdays).

565 Puttenham–Seale–The Sands–Sainsburys–Roman Way–Farnham (Mondays to Fridays in this direction only).

688 Milford–Royal Common–Elstead–Cock Hill–Elstead–Puttenham–Seale–The Sands–Waverley Abbey School–Elstead (St. James' School) (Schooldays).

698 Tongham–Ash Green–Ash Station–Ash Wharf–Shawfields–Ash–Tongham–Runfold–Crooksbury–Waverley Abbey School (Schooldays).

10.1.03: All withdrawn and taken over by Countryliner and Thames Bus.

300

24.7.10: Park and Ride service: Merrow Park and Ride site–Epsom Road–Guildford (Mondays to Saturdays). Most Monday–Friday journeys also ran via Boxgrove Road and London Road. Previously operated by First Beeline.

17.9.11: Diverted via Epsom Road to.from Guildford for all journeys.

31.8.13 Withdrawn and taken over by Stagecoach Hants & Surrey.

823

21.3.11: Grange Park–Stoughton–Bellfields–Woking Road–George Abbot School (Schooldays) Previously operated by Countryliner.

22.7.11: Withdrawn.

APPENDIX 2

List of Safeguard buses and coaches: 1924 – Present Day

Explanation of codes used to describe vehicle bodies:
The standard codes as recognised in most enthusiasts' publications have been used to describe body type and seating capacity.

Prefix:

B	Single deck bus
C	Single deck coach
CH	Double deck coach
Ch	Charabanc (open or with folding canvas roof) with bench seats
DP	Single deck dual purpose vehicle
H	Conventional height double deck bus
M	Minibus

Figures: Seating capacity as quoted

Suffix:

C	Centre entrance
D	Dual entrance
F	Front or forward entrance
R	Rear entrance
T	Toilet compartment

Registration Number(s)	Chassis Manufacturer and Model	Body Manufacturer and Model	Body Type and Seating	Immediate Previous Owner	Date Acquired	Date Out of Fleet	Notes and Subsequent Registrations
?	DAIMLER Y	?	Ch28		/24	?	Originally a lorry chassis. Registration may have been PB9977
?	CHEVROLET LO	REAL	Ch14		/26	/28	Re-bodied 1928 as PH7996 (see below)
?	CHEVROLET LO	REAL	Ch14		/26	/28	Re-bodied 1928 as PH7997 (see below)
?	BERLIET	?	Ch14		/26	?	
PF1837	CHEVROLET LO	REAL	B14F		BY 6/26	/31	Guildford Licence 72, later 49
PF1838	CHEVROLET LO	REAL	B14F		BY 6/26	/31	Guildford Licence 73, later 45
PH4809	CHEVROLET LO (6 WHEEL)	REAL	B20F		10/27	/31	Guildford Licence 46
YW3286	CHEVROLET LO	REAL	C14F		5/28	3/32	Guildford Licence 58
PH7996	CHEVROLET LO	SLOUGH QUALITY	B14F		12/28	/33	Guildford Licence 73
PH7997	CHEVROLET LO	SLOUGH QUALITY	B14F		12/28	/33	Guildford Licence 72
PK7173	CHEVROLET LO	REAL	B14F		3/29	/32	Guildford Licence 87
PK9505	CHEVROLET LO	REAL	C14F		BY 6/29	/32	Guildford Licence 36
PG5320	GRAHAM-DODGE	THURGOOD	B29R		1/30	/34	
HX320	CHEVROLET U	REAL	B14F		6/30	9/34	
HX482	CHEVROLET U	REAL	B14F		6/30	/36	
HX9683	DENNIS 2 TON	REAL	B20F		3/31	12/42	
HX9684	DENNIS 2 TON	REAL	B20F		3/31	9/37	
HX9688	DENNIS GL	REAL	C20F		6/31	/36	
PJ5158	DENNIS LANCET	DUPLE	C32R		3/32	3/49	Re-bodied 1938 Willowbrook B32F
PJ5159	DENNIS LANCET	DUPLE	C32R		4/32	3/49	Re-bodied 1939 Dennis B32F
APD936	DENNIS LANCET	DUPLE	C32R		5/33	3/50	Re-bodied 1940 Dennis B32F
APD937	DENNIS LANCET	DUPLE	C32R		5/33	/46	
CPL205	DENNIS ACE	DENNIS	C20F		8/35	6/50	
DPH990	DENNIS LANCET 6	DUPLE	C32F		3/36	/40	
TV7472	TILLING-STEVENS B39A7	WILLOWBROOK	B32F	TRENT	10/36	11/38	
TV6765	TILLING-STEVENS B39A7	WILLOWBROOK	B32F	TRENT	1/37	1/39	
GPF66	BEDFORD WTB	WILLMOTT	C26R		3/38	3/54	Re-built 1947 King & Taylor C26F
GY1198	DENNIS ARROW	LONDON LORRIES	C32R	M.T.CO.,LONDON SE14	7/38	6/40	
GY2221	DENNIS LANCET	SHORT	C32R	M.T.CO.,LONDON SE14	7/38	6/40	
JPB125	BEDFORD WTB	WILLMOTT	C26F		7/39	3/52	
DMX4	DENNIS LANCET	DUPLE	C32C	?	7/40	/40	
CRK801	BEDFORD WTB	DUPLE	C26F	WILSON, WARLINGHAM	9/40	11/50	
UD9615	ALBION PK115	HEAVER	C27F	SPIERS, HENLEY	/40	?	Ownership not confirmed
GY208	DENNIS LANCET	DENNIS	C32R	RIDD, LONDON W6	12/40	/50	Re-bodied 1943 Dennis B32F
AOR76	DENNIS LANCET	DENNIS	C30C	GLIDER & BLUE, BISHOPS WALTHAM	6/41	11/50	
JPK783	BEDFORD OWB	DUPLE	B32F		12/42	1/51	
JPL759	BEDFORD OWB	DUPLE	B32F		/44	11/52	
KPC658	BEDFORD OB	DUPLE	B32F		3/46	10/54	Later B30F
KPE455	BEDFORD OB	DUPLE	B32F		5/46	10/54	Later B30F, then B28F
APX291	DENNIS ACE	WILLMOTT	B20F	MITCHELL, WARNHAM	3/47	12/48	
MPE410	DENNIS LANCET J3	READING	B32F		7/48	10/58	
MPF700	DENNIS LANCET J3	READING	B32F		8/48	10/57	Later B33F
OPA883	VULCAN 6PF	DUTFIELD	C29F		3/50	9/56	
HWA787	GUY ARAB II	WEYMANN	H55R	LANSDOWNE, LONDON E11	4/50	4/52	
EDL445	BEDFORD OB	DUPLE VISTA	C29F	MOSS, SANDOWN	11/50	9/59	
MMY696	BEDFORD OB	DUPLE VISTA	C29F	HALL, HILLINGDON	1/51	10/55	
FHO769	DENNIS LANCET J3	WADHAM	C32F	HUTFIELD, GOSPORT	12/51	11/52	
JTU97	DENNIS LANCET J3	YEATES	C35F	ROBERTS, CREWE	6/52	1/54	
ENT581	DENNIS LANCET J3	DUPLE	F35F	SALOPIA,WHITCHURCH	11/52	10/56	
FAW532	BEDFORD OB	DUPLE VISTA	C29F	SALOPIA,WHITCHURCH	11/52	10/60	
KGK419	BEDFORD OB	DUPLE VISTA	C29F	WREN, LONDON NW9	2/54	3/57	
GDW981	BEDFORD SB	DUPLE VEGA	C33F	ALPHA, BRIGHTON	3/54	2/59	
UPK615	BEDFORD SBO	DUPLE MIDLAND	B39F		6/54	1/61	

Reg	Chassis	Body	Seating	Previous Owner	In	Out	Notes
VPJ750	BEDFORD SBO	DUPLE MIDLAND	B39F		10/54	11/61	
KCG974	BEDFORD SB	DUPLE VEGA	C35F	COLISEUM, SOUTHAMPTON	10/55	2/60	
200APB	AEC RELIANCE MU3RV	BURLINGHAM	B44F		3/56	10/62	
200BPG	AEC RELIANCE MU3RV	BURLINGHAM	B44F		10/56	5/64	
MHO627	BEDFORD SBG	DUPLE VEGA	C38F	COLISEUM, SOUTHAMPTON	3/57	11/61	
197DPK	AEC RELIANCE MU3RV	BURLINGHAM	B45F		10/57	3/66	
MXL746	BEDFORD SB	DUPLE VEGA	C33F	PHILLIPS, CINDERFORD	5/58	6/61	
PAA207	BEDFORD SBG	DUPLE VEGA	C41F	COLISEUM, SOUTHAMPTON	10/58	4/62	
PCG293	BEDFORD SBG	DUPLE VEGA	C41F	COLISEUM, SOUTHAMPTON	3/59	10/60	
250LPB	BEDFORD SB1	DUPLE MIDLAND	B35F		9/59	1/64	
RHO553	BEDFORD SBG	DUPLE VEGA	C41F	COLISEUM, SOUTHAMPTON	10/59	5/62	
144PPH	BEDFORD SB3	PLAXTON EMBASSY	C41F		6/60	1/63	
630SPH	BEDFORD SB8	DUPLE MIDLAND	B41F		1/61	5/66	
310TPK	BEDFORD SB1	PLAXTON EMBASSY	C41F		5/61	4/65	
739UPF	BEDFORD SB1	PLAXTON EMBASSY	C41F		7/61	10/65	
699VPL	BEDFORD SB8	DUPLE MIDLAND	B41F		9/61	4/70	
VCE520	BEDFORD SB1	DUPLE SUPER VEGA	C41F	HARVEY, CAMBRIDGE	12/61	1/64	
XCG712	BEDFORD SB1	DUPLE SUPER VEGA	C41F	RICKETTS, BAGSHOT	4/62	6/64	
729XPF	BEDFORD SB5	DUPLE SUPER VEGA	C41F		4/62	4/66	
5389PL	AEC RELIANCE 2MU3RV	WILLOWBROOK	B45F		9/62	11/71	
1920PJ	BEDFORD SB5	DUPLE BELLA VEGA	C41F		3/63	12/68	
1637PF	AEC RELIANCE 2U3RA	WILLOWBROOK	B53F		9/63	11/69	
119GBM	BEDFORD VAS1	DUPLE BELLA VISTA	C29F	COOK, BIGGLESWADE	10/63	4/66	
APA46B	AEC RELIANCE 2U3RA	WILLOWBROOK	B53F		12/63	11/69	
BPC299B	BEDFORD SB5	DUPLE BELLA VEGA	C41F		5/64	12/68	
BPC300B	BEDFORD SB5	DUPLE BELLA VEGA	C41F		5/64	/69	
EPH189B	AEC RELIANCE 2U3RA	WILLOWBROOK	B53F		10/64	3/71	
HPB951C	BEDFORD VAL14	PLAXTON PANORAMA	C52F		3/65	12/68	
GPC58C	BEDFORD VAL14	PLAXTON PANORAMA	C52F	COOKE, STOUGHTON	3/66	3/68	
GPD233C	BEDFORD VAS1	PLAXTON EMBASSY	C29F	COOKE, STOUGHTON	3/66	11/69	
472JHO	BEDFORD SB5	PLAXTON EMBASSY	C41F	COOKE, STOUGHTON	3/66	2/67	
644HAA	BEDFORD J2SZ2	PLAXTON EMBASSY	C18F	COOKE, STOUGHTON	3/66	7/68	
201HOU	BEDFORD VAS1	PLAXTON EMBASSY	C24F	COOKE, STOUGHTON	3/66	5/67	
LPB238D	BEDFORD VAM14	DUPLE MIDLAND	B45F		3/66	3/71	
LPH515D	BEDFORD VAM5	PLAXTON PANORAMA	C45F		3/66	2/73	
LPH516D	BEDFORD VAM5	PLAXTON PANORAMA	C45F		3/66	2/73	
MPJ498D	BEDFORD VAM14	DUPLE VICEROY	C45F		10/66	5/72	
PPK735E	BEDFORD VAM14	DUPLE VICEROY	C45F		2/67	5/72	
VCE520	BEDFORD SB1	DUPLE SUPER VEGA	C41F	BAKER, FARNHAM	3/67	10/67	2nd time owned
OPF345E	BEDFORD VAS5	DUPLE BELLA VISTA	C29F		5/67	11/71	
SPK749F	BEDFORD SB5	PLAXTON PANORAMA	C41F		12/67	4/72	
SPK750F	BEDFORD VAL70	DUPLE VICEROY	C52F		12/67	12/71	
UPD381F	BEDFORD VAM70	DUPLE VICEROY	C45F		3/68	4/73	
UPL311F	BEDFORD J2SZ10	PLAXTON EMBASSY	C20F		7/68	6/71	
WPF872G	BEDFORD VAL70	PLAXTON PANORAMA ELITE	C52F		12/68	6/74	
WPK365G	BEDFORD VAM70	PLAXTON PANORAMA ELITE	C45F		1/69	5/75	
WPK366G	BEDFORD VAM70	PLAXTON PANORAMA ELITE	C45F		3/69	4/75	
UAA751H	BEDFORD VAM70	WILLOWBROOK	B45F		11/69	6/74	
UAA752H	BEDFORD VAM70	WILLOWBROOK	B45F		11/69	4/75	
UAA753H	BEDFORD SB5	DUPLE VEGA 31	C41F		11/69	3/12	
UAA754H	BEDFORD VAS5	DUPLE VISTA 25	C29F		11/69	10/73	
UOR603H	BEDFORD VAM70	WILLOWBROOK	B45F		3/70	8/74	
SHP765G	BEDFORD VAL70	DUPLE VICEROY	C53F	SHAW, COVENTRY	6/70	2/73	
266BLB	BEDFORD SB8	DUPLE SUPER VEGA	C41F	BORDERLINE, BRACKLEY	6/70	11/71	
EPH241J	BEDFORD YRQ	PLAXTON PANORAMA ELITE	C45F		1/71	3/76	
EPH242J	AEC RELIANCE 6MU4R	PLAXTON PANORAMA ELITE	C45F		1/71	9/74	
EPK106J	AEC RELIANCE 6MU4R	WILLOWBROOK	B51F		3/71	3/76	
EPK107J	AEC RELIANCE 6MU4R	WILLOWBROOK	B51F		3/71	3/76	

Reg	Chassis	Body	Seating	Notes	In	Out	Extra
FPC15J	AEC RELIANCE 6MU4R	WILLOWBROOK	B51F		4/71	9/77	
GPA112J	AEC RELIANCE 6MU4R	PLAXTON PANORAMA ELITE	C45F		6/71	8/75	
HPE200K	AEC RELIANCE 6MU4R	PLAXTON PANORAMA ELITE	C45F		1/72	9/77	
HPJ999K	AEC RELIANCE 6U3ZR	PLAXTON PANORAMA ELITE	C51F		1/72	10/76	
JPJ100K	BEDFORD VAS5	PLAXTON PANORAMA	C29F		2/72	2/75	
KPD179K	BEDFORD YRQ	PLAXTON PANORAMA ELITE	C41F		3/72	4/75	
KPL776K	BEDFORD YRQ	PLAXTON PANORAMA ELITE	C41F		4/72	1/76	
LPD30K	FORD R1114	DUPLE VICEROY	C53F		5/72	10/73	
OPK131L	BEDFORD YRT	DUPLE DOMINANT	C53F		2/73	2/75	
OPK132L	BEDFORD YRT	DUPLE DOMINANT	C53F		2/73	8/75	
RPA112L	BEDFORD YRT	DUPLE DOMINANT	C53F		5/73	6/76	
RPA113L	BEDFORD YRT	DUPLE DOMINANT	C53F		5/73	10/76	
TPH153M	BEDFORD YRT	DUPLE DOMINANT	C53F		10/73	9/77	
TPJ780M	BEDFORD YRT	DUPLE DOMINANT	C53F		10/73	2/76	
VPE172M	BEDFORD YRQ	DUPLE DOMINANT	C45F		3/74	9/77	
VPF41M	BEDFORD YRQ	DUPLE DOMINANT	C45F		4/74	11/78	
VPF42M	LEYLAND LEOPARD PSU3B/4R	WILLOWBROOK	B53F		5/74	4/81	
WPA153M	BEDFORD YRQ	DUPLE DOMINANT	C45F		6/74	2/78	
GPA853N	BEDFORD YRQ	DUPLE DOMINANT	B45F		12/74	2/80	
GPA854N	BEDFROD YRQ	DUPLE DOMINANT	C45F		12/74	3/78	
GPA855N	BEDFORD YRQ	DUPLE DOMINANT	C41F		12/74	5/79	
HPG29N	LEYLAND LEOPARD PSU3B/4R	DUPLE DOMINANT	C49F		2/75	10/79	
HPG30N	LEYLAND LEOPARD PSU3B/4R	DUPLE DOMINANT	C49F		3/75	10/78	
HPG31N	LEYLAND LEOPARD PSU3B/4R	DUPLE DOMINANT	B53F		5/75	1/82	
KPH626P	LEYLAND LEOPARD PSU3C/4R	DUPLE DOMINANT	C49F		8/75	1/81	
KPH627P	BEDFORD YRQ	DUPLE DOMINANT	C45F		9/75	2/80	
FLB482C	FORD THAMES 570E	DUPLE TROOPER	C41F	CONWAY HUNT, OTTERSHAW	12/75	1/76	Not operated
DMJ488D	FORD R226	DUPLE MARINER	C52F	CONWAY HUNT, OTTERSHAW	12/75	1/76	Not operated
KBL110P	FORD TRANSIT	DEANSGATE	M12	REED, MAIDENHEAD	2/76	8/78	
MPG151P	LEYLAND LEOPARD PSU3C/4R	DUPLE DOMINANT	B53F		4/76	6/88	
MPG152P	BEDFORD YMT	DUPLE DOMINANT	C53F		4/76	10/78	
MPG153P	LEYLAND LEOPARD PSU3C/4R	DUPLE DOMINANT	B53F		4/76	10/82	
MPG154P	BEDFORD YMT	DUPLE DOMINANT	C53F		5/76	10/78	
HRN684G	AEC RELIANCE 6MU4R	PLAXTON PANORAMA ELITE	C45F	PREMIER, PRESTON	5/76	10/76	
OPC25R	BEDFORD YMT	DUPLE DOMINANT	C53F		10/76	6/80	
OPC26R	LEYLAND LEOPARD PSU3C/4R	DUPLE DOMINANT	B53F		10/76	5/88	
PPE658R	BEDFORD YMT	DUPLE DOMINANT	C53F		3/77	9/80	
PPE659R	BEDFORD YMT	DUPLE DOMINANT	C53F		3/77	1/81	
TPL166S	BEDFORD YMT	DUPLE DOMINANT	B53F		8/77	7/87	
TPL167S	BEDFORD YMT	DUPLE DOMINANT	C53F		9/77	/82	
UPH109S	LEYLAND LEOPARD PSU3E/4R	PLAXTON SUPREME	C49F		11/77	4/84	
TPJ273S	BEDFORD YLQ	DUPLE DOMINANT	C29F		2/78	/83	
TPJ274S	BEDFORD YLQ	DUPLE DOMINANT	C41F		4/78	3/82	
XPH539T	FORD TRANSIT	TRICENTROL	M12		7/78	11/81	
VDV97S	BEDFORD VAS5	DUPLE DOMINANT	C29F	SEWARD, DALWOOD	12/78	5/80	
YPB837T	BEDFORD YMT	PLAXTON SUPREME	C53F		1/79	5/82	
YPB838T	BEDFORD YMT	PLAXTON SUPREME	C53F		2/79	5/83	
YPB839T	LEYLAND LEOPARD PSU3E/4R	PLAXTON SUPREME	C49F		2/79	12/85	
DPD33T	BEDFORD YLQ	DUPLE DOMINANT	C45F		5/79	4/87	
FPA584V	LEYLAND LEOPARD PSU3E/4R	PLAXTON SUPREME	C49F		10/79	3/86	
GPG342V	LEYLAND LEOPARD PSU3E/4R	DUPLE DOMINANT	B53F		2/80	2/94	
AJD164T	LEYLAND LEOPARD PSU3E/4R	PLAXTON SUPREME	C45F	GLENTON, LONDON SE15	5/80	BY 7/84	
JPC783V	BEDFORD YMT	PLAXTON SUPREME	C53F		5/80	BY 12/84	
LPA443W	BEDFORD YMT	PLAXTON SUPREME	C53F		9/80	3/85	
NPD689W	LEYLAND LEOPARD PSU3F/5R	DUPLE DOMINANT	B53F		2/81	9/92	
NPD690W	BEDFORD YMT	PLAXTON SUPREME	C53F		2/81	11/85	
NPG266W	BEDFORD YMT	PLAXTON SUPREME	C53F		3/81	6/85	
SPH13X	FORD TRANSIT	TRICENTROL	M12		11/81	8/86	

Reg	Chassis	Body	Seating	Previous Owner	From	To / Notes
TPA968X	LEYLAND LEOPARD PSU3E/4R	DUPLE DOMINANT	B53F		12/81	9/92
UPG349X	LEYLAND TIGER TRCTL11/3R	PLAXTON SUPREME	C53F		4/82	12/86
YPD217Y	LEYLAND LEOPARD PSU3G/4R	DUPLE DOMINANT	B53F		11/82	2/94
APF617Y	BEDFORD YNT	PLAXTON PARAMOUNT	C53F		4/83	10/90
BPC227Y	BEDFORD YNT	PLAXTON PARAMOUNT	C49F		5/83	11/89
A60FPD	BEDFORD YNT	PLAXTON PARAMOUNT	C49F		1/84	9/88
A61FPD	BEDFORD YNT	PLAXTON PARAMOUNT	C53F		4/84	1/87
A60GPL	MERCEDES BENZ L608D	REEVE BURGESS	C19F		5/84	5/98
A62HPG	LEYLAND TIGER TRCTL11/3R	PLAXTON PARAMOUNT	C53F		7/84	1/03
B717MPC	LEYLAND TIGER TRCTL11/3R	DUPLE CARIBBEAN	C51F		12/84	12/89
UTN956Y	LEYLAND TIGER TRCTL11/3R	PLAXTON PARAMOUNT	C51F	MOORDALE, NEWCASTLE	6/85	12/87
UGB14R	AEC RELIANCE 6U3ZR	DUPLE DOMINANT	B53F	TILLINGBOURNE, CRANLEIGH	9/85	12/87
A203RUR	LEYLAND TIGER TRCTL11/3R	PLAXTON PARAMOUNT	C53F	LEYLAND DEMONSTRATOR	10/85	12/90
C164SPB	LEYLAND TIGER TRBTL11/2R	DUPLE DOMINANT	B53F		11/85	11/01
C270TPL	LEYLAND TIGER TRCTL11/3RZ	PLAXTON PARAMOUNT	C50F		3/86	10/93 DSK560,then C933VPM
D123HML	MERCEDES BENZ L608D	REEVE BURGESS	C19F		8/86	9/93
KUS244Y	LEYLAND TIGER TRCTL11/2R	DUPLE DOMINANT	B51F	HUTCHISON, OVERTOWN	10/86	11/01
B906SPR	VOLVO B10M-61	PLAXTON PARAMOUNT	C53F	EXCELSIOR, BOURNEMOUTH	11/86	3/96
B907SPR	VOLVO B10M-61	PLAXTON PARAMOUNT	C53F	EXCELSIOR, BOURNEMOUTH	11/86	3/96
D159HML	MERCEDES BENZ 609D	REEVE BURGESS	B20F		4/87	3/96
D165HML	LEYLAND LYNX LX112TL	LEYLAND	B49F		6/87	6/96
C105AFX	VOLVO B10M-61	PLAXTON PARAMOUNT	C49F	EXCELSIOR, BOURNEMOUTH	10/87	2/97 Later C53F
E51MMT	LEYLAND LYNX LX112TL	LEYLAND	B49F		11/87	6/96
E297OMG	LEYLAND LYNX LX112L	LEYLAND	B49F		5/88	9/98
E298OMG	LEYLAND LYNX LX112L	LEYLAND	B49F		5/88	9/98
F296RMH	VOLVO B10M-46	PLAXTON PARAMOUNT	C39F		8/88	2/06 WPF926, sold as F296RMH
159FCG	KASSBOHRER SETRA S215HD	KASSBOHRER SETRA	C47Ft	FARNHAM COACHES, WRECCLESHAM	9/88	2/01 Sold as D230BJB. Later C49F
247FCG	KASSBOHRER SETRA S215HD	KASSBOHRER SETRA	C49Ft	FARNHAM COACHES, WRECCLESHAM	9/88	3/95 Sold as CPE385Y
277FCG	KASSBOHRER SETRA S215HD	KASSBOHRER SETRA	C53F	FARNHAM COACHES, WRECCLESHAM	9/88	BY6/92 Sold as A684JPC
515FCG	KASSBOHRER SETRA S215H	KASSBOHRER SETRA	C53F	FARNHAM COACHES, WRECCLESHAM	9/88	2/95 Sold as WPC202X
531FCG	KASSBOHRER SETRA S215H	KASSBOHRER SETRA	C49Ft	FARNHAM COACHES, WRECCLESHAM	9/88	6/99 Sold as APA672Y
D145HML	LEYLAND TIGER TRCTL11/3R	DUPLE 320	C53F	PAN ATLAS, LONDON W3	11/88	2/93 538FCG, sold as D986UPG
XGS777X	LEYLAND LEOPARD PSU5D/4R	PLAXTON SUPREME	C53F	CHAMBERS, STEVENAGE	4/89	BY1/92
F475WFX	VOLVO B10M-60	PLAXTON PARAMOUNT	C53F	EXCELSIOR, BOURNEMOUTH	10/89	5/03 196FCG, then F488UPB. Later C57F
F474WFX	VOLVO B10M-60	PLAXTON PARAMOUNT	C53F	EXCELSIOR, BOURNEMOUTH	12/89	10/98
F794TBC	TAZ D3200	TAZ DUBRAVA	C49Ft	THANDI, BEARWOOD	1/90	10/92 DSK558, sold as F199UPC
G514EFX	VOLVO B10M-60	PLAXTON PARAMOUNT	C53F	EXCELSIOR, BOURNEMOUTH	10/90	8/10 247FCG, then back to G514EFX
C665UPJ	KASSBOHRER SETRA S215HR	KASSBOHRER SETRA	C49Ft	TOURSWIFT, BIRTLEY	11/90	2/04 DSK559, then 538FCG, sold as C665UPJ
D192ESC	MCW METROLINER DR102	METRO CAMMELL	CH67Ct	KAVANAGH, URLINGFORD	1/91	3/91
D633XVV	VOLKSWAGEN LT55	OPTARE CITY PACER	B25F	LEICESTER CITYBUS	6/91	6/96
G520EFX	VOLVO B10M-60	PLAXTON PARAMOUNT	C53F	EXCELSIOR, BOURNEMOUTH	11/91	8/10 277FCG, then back to G520EFX
H672ATN	TOYOTA HB31R	CAETANO OPTIMO	C21F	ROSE, BROADWAY	8/92	8/01
F437DUG	VOLVO B10M-60	PLAXTON PARAMOUNT	C53F	WALLACE ARNOLD, TORQUAY	9/92	6/00 DSK558, then back to F437DUG
G540LWU	VOLVO B10M-60	PLAXTON PARAMOUNT	C53F	WALLACE ARNOLD, TORQUAY	1/93	6/00 DSK559, then back to G540LWU
K628YPL	DENNIS DART 9.8SDL	PLAXTON POINTER	B40F		6/93	4/03
G122KUB	MERCEDES BENZ 811D	OPTARE STAR RIDER	C29F	BRENTS, WATFORD	8/93	2/03
G515LWU	VOLVO B10M-60	PLAXTON PARAMOUNT	C53F	WALLACE ARNOLD, LEEDS	10/93	12/00 DSK560, sold as G515LWU
L265EPD	DENNIS DART 9.8SDL	PLAXTON POINTER	B40F		1/94	7/03
F623FNA	MERCEDES BENZ 609D	MADE TO MEASURE	B24F	BERRY, STOCKTON	8/94	8/00
F630NNF	KASSBOHRER SETRA S215HD	KASSBOHRER SETRA	C49F	EBDON, SIDCUP	11/94	2/04 515FCG, sold as F630NNF
J745CWT	VOLVO B10M-60	PLAXTON PREMIERE	C50F	WALLACE ARNOLD, TORQUAY	2/95	2/03 247FCG, then J745CWT, then DSK558, sold as J745CWT
J705CWT	VOLVO B10M-60	PLAXTON PREMIERE	C48Ft	WALLACE ARNOLD, TORQUAY	3/95	3/05 196FCG, then J705CWT, then 247FCG, sold as J705CWT. Later C50F
N561UPF	VOLVO B10M-62	PLAXTON PREMIERE	C49Ft		2/96	1/09 531FCG, then back to N561UPF
N562UPF	DENNIS JAVELIN 12SDA	PLAXTON PREMIERE	C53F		2/96	9/08 DSK560, then back to N562UPF
E169OMU	VOLVO B10M-61	DUPLE 340	C49Ft	KAVANAGH, URLINGFORD	3/96	4/99
M295THD	MERCEDES BENZ 814D	PLAXTON BEAVER	C33F	HANSON COACH, HALIFAX	3/96	12/03
C358KEP	NEOPLAN N722	PLAXTON 4000	CH71Ct	DAVIES, SLOUGH	5/96	12/01 WPF926, sold as C358KEP
J807FNJ	DENNIS JAVELIN 11SDL	PLAXTON PARAMOUNT	C49F	COURTLANDS, HORLEY	5/96	6/01 Later C53F

Reg	Chassis	Body	Seating	Previous Owner	In	Out/Notes
F40LTO	VOLVO B10M-60	PLAXTON PARAMOUNT	C57F	TURNER, BRISTOL	8/96	6/02
G89KUB	MERCEDES BENZ 811D	OPTARE STAR RIDER	B29F	METROLINE	12/96	9/02
P46GPG	VOLVO B10M-62	VAN HOOL ALIZEE	C53F		2/97	CURRENT DSK559. Later C49Ft, then back to C53F
M622RCP	EOS E180Z	EOS 90	C47Ft	LANDTOURERS, EWSHOT	3/97	12/00 247FCG, sold as M622RCP. Later C49Ft
M623RCP	EOS E180Z	EOS 90	C47Ft	LANDTOURERS, EWSHOT	3/97	12/05 196FCG, sold as M623RCP. Later C49Ft
M624RCP	EOS E180Z	EOS 90	C47Ft	LANDTOURERS, EWSHOT	3/97	12/00 531FCG, sold as M624RCP
M625RCP	EOS E180Z	EOS 90	C47Ft	LANDTOURERS, EWSHOT	3/97	12/05 277FCG, sold as M625RCP. Later C49Ft
MIW8529	MCW METROLINER DR130	METRO CAMMELL	CH72Dt	LOGANS TOURS, SOUTHFLEET	9/97	9/99
XHY378	NEOPLAN N122	NEOPLAN SKYLINER	CH75Ct	MCTAGGART, GREENOCK	11/97	11/98 Sold as A385XGG
L967RUB	TOYOTA HZB50R	CAETANO OPTIMO	C21F	APPLEGATE, NEWPORT	4/98	2/06
S503UAK	DENNIS JAVELIN SFD721	PLAXTON PREMIERE	C57F		8/98	CURRENT
N611WND	DENNIS DART 9.8SDL	NORTHERN COUNTIES	B39F	METEOR, LONDON W1	9/98	1/09
M388KVR	DENNIS DART 9.8SDL	NORTHERN COUNTIES	B39F	WEST MIDLANDS	9/98	4/06
F617CWJ	NEOPLAN N122	NEOPLAN SKYLINER	CH73Ct	ROFFEY, FLIMWELL	10/98	2/03 XHY378, sold as F617CWJ
M974NFU	KASSBOHRER SETRA S250	KASSBOHRER SETRA	C53F	Q DRIVE, BATTERSEA	4/99	9/07 159FCG, sold as M974NFU
L356YNR	DENNIS JAVELIN 12SDA	PLAXTON PREMIERE	C53F	SPENCER, NEW OLLERTON	9/99	5/02
H577MOC	DENNIS DART 8.5SDL	CARLYLE DARTLINE	B28F	WARNER, TEWKESBURY	1/00	8/11
P970HWF	DENNIS JAVELIN SFD531	NEOPLAN TRANSLINER	C49Ft	BUSBRIDGE, ASHFORD	BY3/00	5/02 DSK559, sold as P970HWF
W354EOL	KASSBOHRER SETRA S250	KASSBOHRER SETRA	C48Ft		3/00	10/11 538FCG
V943DNB	DENNIS DART SLF SFD612	PLAXTON POINTER	B29F	CONNEX BUS	8/00	8/01
V946DNB	DENNIS DART SLF SFD612	PLAXTON POINTER	B29F	TRENT	8/00	1/02
R774WOB	DENNIS JAVELIN SFD721	PLAXTON PREMIERE	C53F	FLIGHTS, BIRMINGHAM	12/00	12/03
Y161HWE	MAN 18.350	NEOPLAN TRANSLINER	C47Ft		12/00	5/07 Later C53F
Y162HWE	MAN 18.350	NEOPLAN TRANSLINER	C47Ft		12/00	9/07 Later C53F
W417HOB	MERCEDES BENZ 0404-15R	HISPANO VITO	C49Ft	AUSTIN, EARLESTON	2/01	3/12 515FCG
R433FWT	VOLVO B10M-62	PLAXTON PREMIERE	C53F	WALLACE ARNOLD, LEEDS	8/01	CURRENT
X307CBT	OPTARE L1150	OPTARE EXCEL	B39F	TILLINGBOURNE, CRANLEIGH	9/01	CURRENT
X308CBT	OPTARE L1150	OPTARE EXCEL	B39F	TILLINGBOURNE, CRANLEIGH	9/01	CURRENT
W203YAP	MERCEDES BENZ 0814D	PLAXTON CHEETAH	C29F	AIRLINKS	9/01	7/13
FXU355	NEOPLAN N122	NEOPLAN SKYLINER	CH77Ct	TRATHEN, PLYMOUTH	11/01	9/04
200APB	AEC RELIANCE MU3RV	BURLINGHAM	B44F	REXQUOTE, BISHOPS LYDEARD	1/02	CURRENT Second time owned
YL51ZTK	OPTARE ALERO	OPTARE	B12F		1/02	6/02
R410EOS	VOLVO B10M-62	VAN HOOL ALIZEE	C53F	PARK, HAMILTON	5/02	CURRENT DSK558. Later C49Ft, then back to C53F
CN51XNO	VOLVO B7R	PLAXTON PRIMA	C57F	BEBB, LLANTWIT FARDRE	5/02	10/09 196FCG, sold as CN51XNO
R398EOS	VOLVO B10M-62	VAN HOOL ALIZEE	C53F	PARK, HAMILTON	6/02	CURRENT XHY378. Later C49Ft, then back to C53F
VU02TTJ	DENNIS DART SLF SFD6B	PLAXTON POINTER	B29F		4/02	CURRENT
S132PGB	VOLVO B10M-62	VAN HOOL ALIZEE	C49Ft	CLYDE COAST, ARDROSSAN	11/02	CURRENT WPF926. Later C53F
T530EUB	VOLVO B10M-62	PLAXTON PREMIERE	C49Ft	WALLACE ARNOLD, LEEDS	2/03	CURRENT DSK560, then back to T530EUB
RX03XKH	DENNIS JAVELIN SFD741	PLAXTON PROFILE	C70F		3/03	CURRENT
YJ03UMM	OPTARE L1180	OPTARE EXCEL	B41F		4/03	CURRENT
W257UGX	KASSBOHRER SETRA S315GT	KASSBOHRER SETRA	C53F	PULLMANOR, LONDON SE5	5/03	3/12 159FCG, then back to W257UGX
W209YAP	MERCEDES BENZ 0814D	PLAXTON CHEETAH	C29F	NATIONAL EXPRESS	12/03	9/08 Last coach in Farnham lilac/white livery
Y748HWT	VOLVO B10M-62	PLAXTON PARAGON	C48Ft	WALLACE ARNOLD, LEEDS	12/03	CURRENT 196FCG, then back to Y748HWT
W295UGX	KASSBOHRER SETRA S315GT	KASSBOHRER SETRA	C48Ft	PULLMANOR, LONDON SE5	1/04	12/06
Y758HWT	VOLVO B10M-62	PLAXTON PARAGON	C53F	WALLACE ARNOLD, LEEDS	9/04	CURRENT 531FCG
YN05HUY	VOLVO B12M	PLAXTON PARAGON	C53F		3/05	CURRENT Later C57F
YN04WTL	VOLVO B12M	PLAXTON PARAGON	C49Ft	LOGAN, DUNLOY	12/05	CURRENT 247FCG. Later C53F
YN04WTM	VOLVO B12M	PLAXTON PARAGON	C49Ft	LOGAN, DUNLOY	12/05	CURRENT 277FCG. Later C53F
YJ06FXM	OPTARE X1130	OPTARE TEMPO	B37F		4/06	CURRENT
BX56VTM	MERCEDES BENZ OC510	MERCEDES TOURINO	C36F		12/06	CURRENT
FY03WZN	MERCEDES BENZ 1223L	FERQUI	C39F	CHIVERS, ELSTEAD	2/07	CURRENT
WA07KXX	VOLVO B12B	VAN HOOL ALICRON	C53F		5/07	CURRENT
WA57CYY	VOLVO B12B	VAN HOOL ALICRON	C53F		9/07	CURRENT
WN57BWW	VOLVO B12M	PLAXTON PARAGON	C57F		9/07	CURRENT
WA58EOO	VOLVO B12B	VAN HOOL ALICRON	C49Ft		9/08	CURRENT
MX58ABF	OPTARE V1100	OPTARE VERSA	B41F		10/08	CURRENT
YN58NCC	VOLVO B12M	PLAXTON PANTHER	C53Ft		1/09	CURRENT
YN58NDD	VOLVO B12M	PLAXTON PANTHER	C53Ft		1/09	CURRENT

YJ10EZT	OPTARE V1110	OPTARE VERSA	B38F		5/10	CURRENT
LK06BWB	DENNIS DART SLF SFD4D	EAST LANCS MYLLENNIUM	B39F	FIRST BEELINE	7/10	9/13
LK07CBO	DENNIS DART SLF SFD4D	EAST LANCS MYLLENNIUM	B39F	FIRST BEELINE	7/10	9/13
LK07CBU	DENNIS DART SLF SFD4D	EAST LANCS MYLLENNIUM	B39F	FIRST BEELINE	7/10	9/13
YJ60LRO	OPTARE V1110	OPTARE VERSA	B38F		1/11	CURRENT
GM57GSM	VOLVO B12B	VAN HOOL ALIZEE	C49Ft	MAYNE, BUCKIE	1/11	CURRENT
WA06CDZ	VOLVO B12M	VAN HOOL ALIZEE	C57F	CHALFONT, SOUTHALL	2/11	CURRENT
SN09JUV	VOLVO B12B	VAN HOOL ALIZEE	C49Ft	AAA, KIRKNEWTON	11/11	CURRENT
SN09JUW	VOLVO B12B	VAN HOOL ALIZEE	C49Ft	AAA, KIRKNEWTON	11/11	CURRENT
SN09JUX	VOLVO B12B	VAN HOOL ALIZEE	C53F	AAA, KIRKNEWTON	11/11	CURRENT
SN60FMO	VOLVO B7R	PLAXTON PROFILE	C70F	ALLAN, GOREBRIDGE	4/12	CURRENT
YD63UZJ	OPTARE V1110	OPTARE VERSA	DP37F		10/13	CURRENT

APPENDIX 3

Company Personnel – November 2013

Directors

Andrew Halliday – Managing Director
David Newman
Therese Hunter
Jane Newman
Mark Newman

Managers and Administrators

Brett Lambley – Engineering Manager
Matthew Tighe – Operations Manager
Heidi Millar – Assistant Operations Manager
Maureen Guyan – Assistant Operations Manager
Linda Chambers – Sales Manager
Sue Gallagher – Sales Manager
Eddie Russell – Financial Controller

Recognition is given to the following current members of staff who have completed five years or more continuous service at 1 November 2013:

Name	Years of Continuous Service
Peter Pearson	26
Jason Hallewell*	26
Linda Chambers	24
Richard Parratt	22
Jane Newman	19
Allan Ford	19
Richard Kirwin*	18
Gordon Lambley	16
John Lake	16
Brett Lambley	15
Chico Luongo*	14
Andrew Halliday	13
Nigel Cotton	12
Darren Cooper	11
Scott Napier	8
Eddie Russell	8
Steve Page	8
Heidi Millar	7
Dave Maddams	7
Peter Birch	6
Andrew Norris	6
Andy Wells	6
Sue Gallagher	6
Malcolm Toghill	6
Dave Goodyear	5
Darren Cartwright	5
Roy Cooke	5

Many of the staff listed have served the Company for more years than shown, albeit not continuously.
* Denotes part-time member of staff

While this list shows current members of staff with long service, there have been numerous other members of staff that have, in the past, had long periods of employment. Some of these people are mentioned in the text, but we regret that records are not accurate enough for a comprehensive list to be published. However, the Company wishes to acknowledge their contribution to its success over the past ninety years.

APPENDIX 4

From the start of operations, through to the 1950s, Safeguard used the ubiquitous Bell Punch-style tickets. Packs of these of the various fare values were put into the hand-held wooden racks used by conductors and taken out as required, before a small hole was made at the appropriate printed Fare Stage with a punch machine.

Ticket no. G7267 dates from the formative years of the business and interestingly shows the proprietor as H. Newman. V5177, B5893, S9456 and H8619 are from the 1930s after the formation of the limited company, while Hf5933 is probably from the early 1950s after the telephone number changed from 1103 to 61103.

(tickets from *Roger Atkinson* and *John King*)

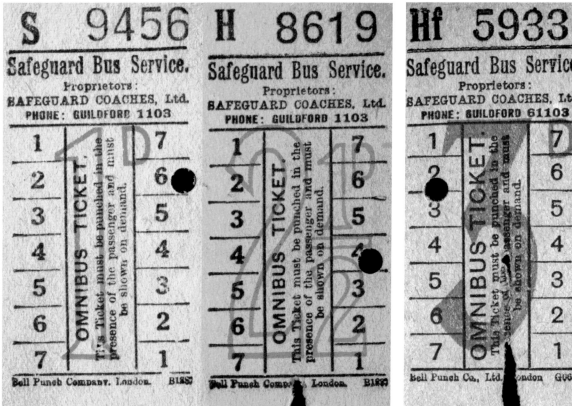

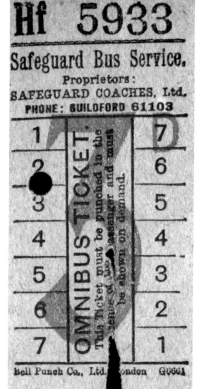

From the late 1950s, the traditional punch-style tickets were replaced with 'Ultimate' tickets, with rolls of tickets with limited different fare values being dispensed from a machine by pushing down small levers.

If these tickets were issued as depicted, they would have been for fares of one shilling, 5 old pence, 3 old pence and 11 old pence, or alternatively, for two passengers at the fare value shown on each individual ticket.

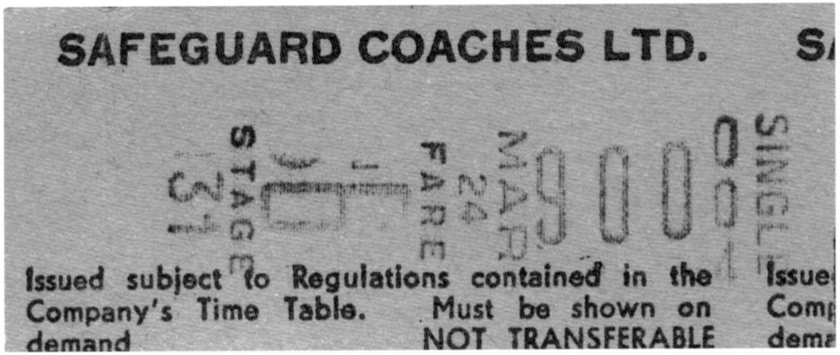

SAFEGUARD COACHES LTD.

STAGE 34   FARE   MAR 24   SINGLE 0001   9000

Issued subject to Regulations contained in the Company's Time Table. Must be shown on demand. NOT TRANSFERABLE.

During the 1960s, Setright roll ticket machines were used alongside Ultimate and later as the only system employed. The fare and other specific details were printed onto the ticket inside the machine.

During the 1970s, by when many journeys were one-man operated, a number of Almex machines were purchased, issuing small square tickets printed within, although the remaining conductors continued to use Setright tickets until 1981.

The manual Almex machines remained in use until around 1997 when electronic Almex A90 machines were introduced. These were replaced from August 2009 by electronic Wayfarer TGX150 machines.

Safeguard Coaches

```
Drv     210   Route       4
Bus       3   Jrny       56
Ticket No           2295
```

Adult Monthly
£43.50

Friary Bus Stn
To
Southway Corner

Tue, 08 Oct 13 11:36

Expires
Thu, 07 Nov 13

Not transferrable
Retain for inspection
Penalty for misuse
Property of Safeguard

F:3048   M:622542   I:0

Safeguard Coaches

```
Drv     210   Route       4
Bus       3   Jrny       56
Ticket No           2292
```

Adult Single
£1.80

Friary Bus Stn
To
Park Barn Loop

Tue, 08 Oct 13 11:35

Not transferrable
Retain for inspection
Penalty for misuse
Property of Safeguard

F:3048   M:622542   I:0

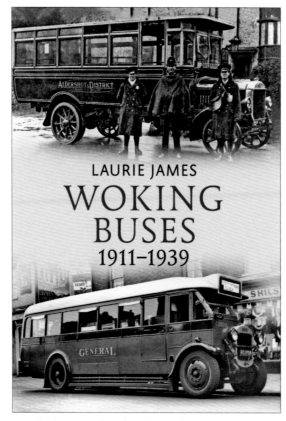